Cells and the origin of life

CAMBRIDGE UNIVERSITY PRESS

Cambridge
New York   New Rochelle
Melbourne   Sydney

Contents

Preface

The Inner London Education Authority's Advanced Biology Alternative Learning (ABAL) project has been developed as a response to changes which have taken place in the organisation of secondary education and the curriculum. The project is the work of a group of biology teachers seconded from ILEA secondary schools. ABAL began in 1978 and since then has undergone extensive trials in schools and colleges of further education. The materials have been produced to help teachers meet the needs of new teaching situations and provide an effective method of learning for students.

Teachers new to A-level teaching or experienced teachers involved in reorganisation of schools due to the changes in population face many problems. These include the sharing of staff and pupils between existing schools and the variety of backgrounds and abilities of pupils starting A-level courses whether at schools, sixth form centres or colleges. Many of the students will be studying a wide range of courses, which in some cases will be a mixture of science, arts and humanities.

The ABAL individualised learning materials offer a guided approach to A-level biology and can be used to form a coherent base in many teaching situations. The materials are organised so that teachers can prepare study programmes suited to their own students. The separation of core and extension work enables the academic needs of all students to be satisfied. Teachers are essential to the success of this course, not only in using their traditional skills, but for organising resources and solving individual problems. They act as a personal tutor, and monitor the progress of each student as he or she proceeds through the course.

The materials aim to help the students develop and improve their personal study skills, enabling them to work more effectively and become more actively involved and responsible for their own learning and assessment. This approach allows the students to develop a sound understanding of fundamental biological concepts.

Acknowledgements

Figures: 2, Courtesy of the Wellcome Institute; 10, 88, 99, A. Langham; 13, W. A. Stevens; 15, 17, 18, 19, 21, 22, 23, 24, 25, 26, 27, 28, 33, 35, 36, 60, 92, 136, Biophoto Associates; 20, 29, 31, J. D. Dodge; 44, D. Williams; 62, S. J. Singer & G. L. Nicolson (1972) *Science*, **175,** 720–731, Copyright 1972 by the American Association for the Advancement of Science; 90, Data from Ursprung & Blum (1916) *Ber. Deutsch Bot. Ges.*, **34,** 525–544.

Examination questions: By permission of the Associated Examining Board, the Oxford and Cambridge Schools Examination Board, the University of London Examining Board, the Joint Matriculation Board and the University of Cambridge Local Examinations Syndicate.

Cover illustration based on a photograph supplied by Science Photo Library.

How to use this unit

This is not a textbook. It is a guide that will help you learn as effectively as possible. As you work through it, you will be directed to practical work, audio-visual resources and other material. There are sections of text in this guide which are to be read as any other book, but much of the guide is concerned with helping you through activities designed to produce effective learning. The following list gives details of the ways in which the unit is organised.

(1) Objectives

Objectives are stated at the beginning of each section. They are important because they tell you what you should be able to do when you have finished working through the section. They should give you extra help in organising your learning. In particular, you should check after working through each section that you can achieve all the stated objectives and that you have notes which cover them all.

(2) Self-assessment questions (*SAQ*)

These are designed to help you think about what you are reading. You should always write down answers to self-assessment questions and then check them immediately with those answers given at the back of this unit. If you do not understand a question and answer, make a note of it and discuss it with your tutor at the earliest opportunity.

(3) Summary assignments

These are designed to help you make notes on the content of a particular section. They will provide a useful collection of revision material. They should therefore be carried out carefully and should be checked by your tutor for accuracy. If you prefer to make notes in your own way, discuss with your tutor whether you should carry out the summary assignments.

(4) Self tests

There are one or more self tests for each section. They should be attempted a few days after you have completed the relevant work and not immediately after. They will help you identify what you have not understood or remembered from a particular section. You can then remedy any weaknesses identified. If you cannot answer any questions and do not understand the answers given, then check with your tutor.

(5) Tutor assesssed work

At intervals through the unit you will meet an instruction to show work to your tutor. This will enable your tutor to monitor your progress through the unit and to see how well you are coping with the material. Your tutor will then know how best to meet your individual needs.

(6) Past examination questions

At various points in the unit you will come across past examination questions. These are only included where they are relevant to the topic under study and have been selected both to improve your knowledge of that topic and also to give you practice in answering examination questions.

(7) Audio-visual material and computer simulations

A number of activities in this unit refer to video cassettes and computer simulations which may be available from your tutor. They deal with topics which cannot be covered easily in text or practical work as well as providing a change from the normal type of learning activities. This should help in motivating you.

(8) Extension work

This work is provided for several reasons: to provide additional material of general interest; to provide more detailed treatment of some topics; to provide more searching questions that will make demands on your powers of thinking and reasoning.

(9) Practicals

These are an integral part of the course and have been designed to lead you to a deeper understanding of the factual material. You will need to organise your time with care so that you can carry out the work suggested in a logical sequence. If your A-level examination requires your practical notebook to be assessed, you must be careful to keep a record of this work in a separate book. A hazard symbol, ☠, is used in the Materials and Procedure sections to mark those substances and procedures which must be treated with particular care!

(10) Discussion

Talking to one another about biological ideas is a helpful activity. To express yourself in your own words, so that others can understand you, forces you to clarify your thoughts. When a sufficient number of your class (at least three, but not more than five) have covered the material indicated by a discussion instruction, you should have a group discussion. Question individuals if what they say is not clear. This is the way that you will both learn and understand.

(11) Programmed learning texts

There are three programmed learning texts in this unit. To use them most effectively, you should take a piece of paper or card (that is a mask) and place it on the first page of the programmed text so that only the text above the first horizontal dividing line is visible. Such an item is called a frame. Each frame will provide you with information and ask you to make a response. When you have done this, move the mask down to reveal the correct answer and the next frame. This procedure should be repeated throughout the programme.

(12) Post-test

A post-test is available from your tutor when you finish this unit. This will be based on past examination questions and will give you an idea of how well you have coped with the material here. It will also indicate which areas you should consolidate before going on to the next unit.

Study and practical skills

The ABAL introductory unit *Inquiry and investigation in biology* introduced certain study and practical skills which will be practised and improved in this unit. These included
(*a*) the QS3R method of note-taking;
(*b*) the construction of graphs, histograms and tables;
(*c*) the analysis of data;
(*d*) the construction and use of keys;
(*e*) drawing of biological specimens;
(*f*) use of the light microscope;
(*g*) the design of practical investigations;
(*h*) comprehension of written reports;
(*i*) discussion groups.

Introduction to this unit

The precise form in which life originated is impossible to define. However, as all living organisms consist of one or more cells, life is believed to have originated in the form of a cell. In this unit you will study the physical and chemical characteristics of cells and consider how they could have originated in the conditions which existed before there was life on Earth.

You will start your study of *Cells and the origin of life* by considering the theory that cells are indeed the basic unit of life – the cell theory. Then you will learn about the chemistry and structure of cells. With this background knowledge, you will next be able to consider how a cell could have been formed in the conditions prevailing at the origin of life. In particular, three aspects of a cell's structure and function will be discussed in detail with respect to its survival in space and time. These are the cell's energy relationships with its environment, the manner in which the cell regulates its exchanges with its environment and how the cell controls its internal activities. Finally, you will look at the growth and reproduction of cells leading to their organisation into co-operating groups in contrast to the view of much of this unit of a cell as an isolated unit of life.

This sequence is outlined in figure 1.

1   The sequence of themes in this unit

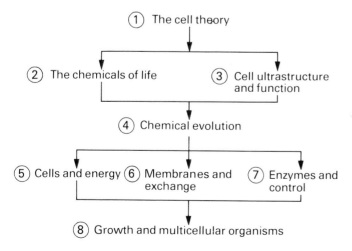

Section 1 The cell theory

1.1 Introduction and objectives

This unit is about cells and their origin and you will start your studies by considering precisely what is meant by the term cell and certain other associated terms.

After completing this section you should be able to do the following.

(a) Explain what is meant by the cell theory.

(b) Name two groups of organisms which are exceptions to the cell theory and explain why they are exceptions.

(c) State what is meant by unicellular and multi-cellular.

(d) List the typical components of a plant and an animal cell.

(e) Define the terms eukaryote and prokaryote.

1.2 The development of cell theory

2   Drawing of cork cells seen by Robert Hooke

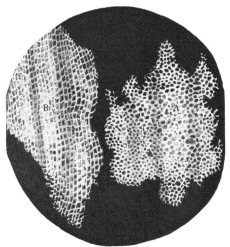

Every living organism is composed of one or more cells. Robert Hooke, a British scientist, was the first

to use the term cell in describing certain structures in a piece of cork, which he observed using a microscope (figure 2). This occurred in 1665; but it was over 150 years later that Dutrochet, a French scientist, realised the significance of the cell as a basic building block and proposed that all living things were made up of cells. This basic principle of cell theory was later supplemented by two further principles. In 1838, Schleiden and Schwann postulated that cells were capable of independent existence, and in 1855 Virchow stated that cells could only arise from pre-existing cells.

SAQ 1 State the three principles of cell theory.

One reason why scientists took so long to recognise the common nature of cells must have been the wide variety of shapes and functions which cells exhibit. This variety is illustrated to some extent in figures 3 and 4 which show different cells from some plants and animals.

The cells illustrated have developed a particular size, shape and chemistry which is suited to the specific function which each performs. Such cells are said to be **specialised** and an organism which is composed of groups of specialised cells is described as **multi-cellular**. This is in contrast to those organisms which consist of only one cell capable of carrying out all the necessary functions which are termed **unicellular**, such as *Amoeba* shown in figure 5. Some biologists

5   A unicellular organism – *Amoeba*

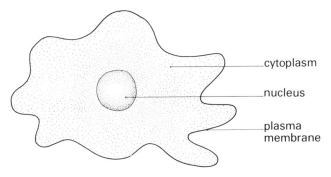

3   Three different plant cells

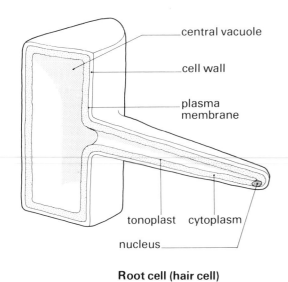

central vacuole

cell wall

plasma membrane

tonoplast   cytoplasm

nucleus

Root cell (hair cell)

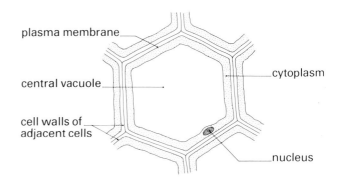

nucleus

plasma membrane

chloroplast

central vacuole

tonoplast

cytoplasm

cell wall

Guard cells around a stoma in a leaf

plasma membrane

central vacuole

cell walls of adjacent cells

cytoplasm

nucleus

Stem cell (parenchyma)

4   Three different animal cells

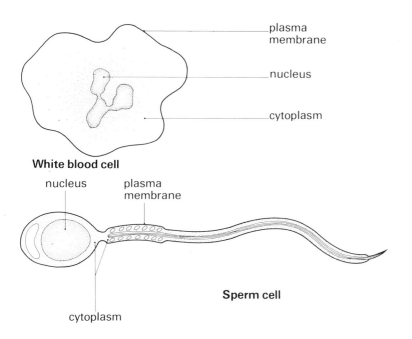

plasma membrane

nucleus

cytoplasm

White blood cell

nucleus   plasma membrane

cytoplasm

Sperm cell

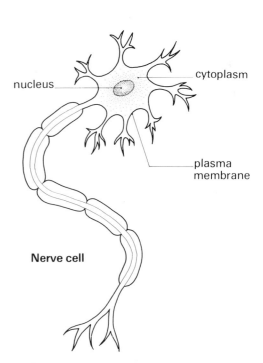

nucleus

cytoplasm

plasma membrane

Nerve cell

prefer to use the term acellular rather than uni-cellular. They emphasise the differences between single-celled organisms and those with many cells, whilst biologists who prefer the term unicellular emphasise the similarities between all cells. Both terms are equally correct, but the term unicellular will be used in this unit.

SAQ 2 Define the terms specialised cell, multicellular organism and unicellular organism.

Despite the wide variety of cells found in various organisms, they do have certain common characteristics which enable them to be recognised as cells. They are all bounded by a plasma membrane and, with the exception of mammalian red blood cells, have a structure called a nucleus which is surrounded by cytoplasm in which various other structures, called organelles, may be found. These common features that are labelled in figures 3, 4 and 5. Plant cells differ from animal cells in certain ways, as can be seen by comparing figure 6 with figures 4 and 5.

6 A generalised plant cell

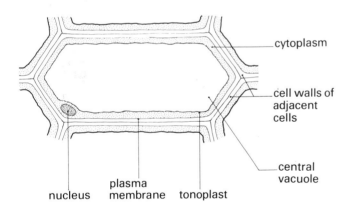

SAQ 3 (*a*) List the similarities and differences between plant and animal cells.
(*b*) Explain what is meant by 'generalised' with reference to the diagram of a plant cell in figure 6.
(*c*) Draw a diagram of a generalised animal cell.

Although the cell theory is generally true, there are certain exceptions amongst the simplest forms of life such as bacteria which are illustrated in figures 7 and 8.

7 A bacterium

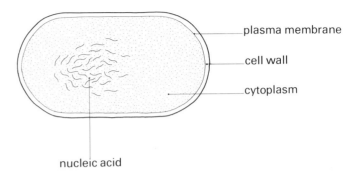

8 A blue-green bacterium

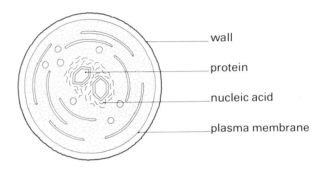

SAQ 4 Using the information in figures 5, 7 and 8 explain
(*a*) why bacteria (including blue-green bacteria) are exceptions to the cell theory;
(*b*) why *Amoeba* is not an exception.

Organisms are classified into two groups, the prokaryotes and eukaryotes. The **eukaryotes** conform with cell theory whilst the **prokaryotes**, though possessing a plasma membrane, cytoplasm and nucleic acid, do not have a distinct nucleus nor any other membrane-bound organelles.

SAQ 5 Give one example each of a prokaryote and a eukaryote.

1.3 Summary assignment 1

The SAQs in this section pick out the essential points. Keep a record of your answers to them as your notes.

Self test 1, page 81, covers section 1 of this unit.

Section 2 The chemicals of life

2.1 Introduction and objectives

Four types of large molecules are universally associated with living material: carbohydrates, proteins, lipids and nucleic acids. The video sequence *The chemicals of life* describes the structure and functions of these type of molecules.

After completing this section you should be able to do the following.

(*a*) Describe the chemical composition, structure, characteristics and major functions of carbohydrates, proteins, lipids and nucleic acids.

(*b*) Explain for each of the four types of molecules listed above
(i) how they are classified, with examples of different types;
(ii) how condensation or hydrolytic reactions are involved in the formation or breaking down of glycosidic, peptide, ester and pentose–phosphate bonds.

(*c*) Name and describe examples of the monomers (monosaccharides, amino acids, triglycerides and nucleotides) which constitute the four molecules listed above.

(*d*) Explain the meaning and significance of the following terms:
aldehyde and keto groupings, ring and open chain forms, amphoteric nature, and specific bonding of bases.

2.2 Pre-knowledge for video sequence 3: *The chemicals of life*

The video sequence *The chemicals of life* has been designed with the assumption that you know what is meant by life and that you have some basic knowledge of chemistry. You should check with your tutor about the need to carry out the work in video

sequences 1 and 2 which deal with *The characteristics of living organisms* and *Chemical foundations* respectively.

AV 1: The characteristics of living organisms

Materials

VCR and monitor
ABAL video sequence: *The characteristics of living organisms*

Procedure

(*a*) Check that you have all the relevant materials for this activity

(*b*) Check that the video cassette is set up ready to show the appropriate audio-visual material – *The characteristics of living organisms*.

(*c*) The film, although short in duration, is the result of many hours of observing and filming living protozoans. As you view it, watch the organisms closely and try to decide what it is about them that makes them 'alive'.

(*d*) Make a list of their various activities that you consider to be characteristic of living organisms.

(*e*) You may find it useful to view the film several times.

(*f*) When you have recorded as many observations as you can, discuss with others in your group whether there are any other processes which are characteristic of life but which could not be observed in the film.

SAQ 6 List the activities characteristic of life which are (*a*) observable and (*b*) not observable in the film. For each activity which is observable, briefly describe the observations you made.

AV 2: Chemical foundations

Materials

VCR and monitor
ABAL video sequence: *Chemical foundations*
Worksheets: 1, 2 and 3

Procedure

(*a*) Check that you have all the relevant materials for this activity.

(*b*) Check that the video cassette is set up ready to show the appropriate sequence – *Chemical foundations*.

(*c*) Start the video and either stop it at the appropriate point to fill in worksheets 1, 2 and 3 as you go or complete the worksheets at the end of the sequence.

(*d*) If you do not understand anything, stop the video, rewind and study the relevant material again before consulting with your tutor.

(*e*) If possible, work through the video and worksheets with a small group and discuss the material amongst yourselves.

AV 3: The chemicals of life

Materials

VCR and monitor
ABAL video sequence: *The chemicals of life*
Worksheets: 4, 5, 6 and 7

Procedure

(*a*) Check that you have all the relevant materials listed above.

(*b*) Check that the video cassette is set up ready to show the appropriate sequence – *The chemicals of life*.

(*c*) Start the sequence and either stop it at the appropriate point to complete worksheets 4, 5, 6 and 7 as you go or complete the worksheets at the end of the sequence.

(*d*) If you do not understand anything, then stop the sequence, rewind and study the relevant material again before consulting with your tutor.

(*e*) If possible, work through the sequence and worksheets with a small group and discuss the material with them.

2.3 Summary assignment 2

Make a list of the seven main characteristics of living organisms and include a brief explanation of each characteristic. (Your worksheets will provide a record of *The chemicals of life*.)

Self test 2, page 81, covers the information contained in the video sequence *The chemicals of life*.

Section 3 Cell ultrastructure and function

3.1 Introduction and objectives

The cell theory is based on observations of structures invisible to the naked eye. If it were not for the extension of the sense of vision made possible by microscopes, such observations could never have been made. In this section you will consider the importance of microscopes and the detail they reveal with respect to a cell's ultrastructure and function.

After completing this section you should be able to do the following.

(a) Describe the ultrastructure and specific function of the following:
nucleolus, chromosome, nuclear and cell membranes, cell wall, cuticle, plasmodesmata, desmosome, cilium, flagellum, basal body, centriole, ribosome, Golgi body, smooth and rough endoplasmic reticulum, chloroplast, mitochondrion, pinocytic and phagocytic vesicles, animal and plant vacuoles.

(b) Identify and draw cell organelles from electron micrographs.

(c) Discuss and give examples of how instruments have been used to extend the human sense of vision.

(d) Calculate the size of a structure given the magnification of an electron micrograph in which is it visible.

Extension

(a) Describe the basic structure and function of an electron microscope.

(b) Explain the limitations of the electron microscope and, in particular, the significance of interpretation of electron micrographs.

3.2 Extending the senses

Scientists can only observe and attempt to understand phenomena by use of their senses. They are, therefore, subject to the limits imposed by the sensitivity and acuity of these senses. Instruments which can extend senses have been responsible for the rapid expansion of knowledge in recent years. The most important of these instruments from the biologist's point of view is the microscope. Figure 9 shows how the light and electron microscopes have

9   The sense extension achieved with light and electron microscopes

	Dimensions			Examples
	mm	μm	nm	
Visible with eye	1.0	1000		giant algal cell
	0.5	500		Amoeba
	0.1	100		
Visible with light microscope	0.05	50		average cell
	0.001	1.0		nucleus
		0.1	100	mitochondrion
Detectable with electron microscope		0.05	50	virus
		0.01	10	cell membrane
		0.001	1.0	large molecule

enabled biologists to see details which were beyond even the imagination of scientists without such aids.

SAQ 7 (*a*) What is the relationship between mm, μm and nm?
(*b*) Give an example of the smallest thing which could be observed with a light microscope and an electron microscope.

Practical A: Cell structure revealed by a compound light microscope

Materials

Microscope and lamp, sterilised wooden spatula (or tongue depressor), Pasteur pipette, microscope slide, cover-slip, fine glass rod, mounted needle, methylene blue solution, filter paper, solution of methyl cellulose, 'isotonic' saline solution, iodine in potassium iodide solution, culture of unicellular organisms

Procedure

(1) Observation of cheek cells

(*a*) Gently scrape the inside of your cheek with the wooden spatula and mount the scrapings in a drop of isotonic saline solution on a microscope slide.

(*b*) Cover with a cover-slip.

(*c*) Observe under low and high power of a compound light microscope. (Full instructions on how to use the microscope are available in the ABAL unit *Inquiry and investigation in biology*.)

(*d*) Record your observations as annotated drawings.

(2) Staining cheek cells (by the irrigation technique)

(*a*) Place a drop of methylene blue solution or iodine in potassium iodide solution on the slide so that it just touches the cover-slip (see figure 10).

(*b*) Place a piece of filter paper in contact with the water on the other side of the cover-slip (see figure 10).

10   Irrigation technique

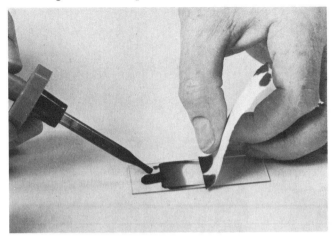

(*c*) The fluid should be withdrawn by the filter paper and replaced by the stain. This is called irrigation.

(*d*) Observe and record as previously.

(*e*) Note and explain why certain regions take up the stain more than others.

(3) Observing unicellular organisms

(*a*) Use the Pasteur pipette to take a sample from the culture.

(*b*) Place a drop of the culture on a clean slide.

(*c*) Dip the glass rod into the methyl cellulose solution and use it to transfer a drop to the slide. Mix with the drop of culture using the rod. The methyl cellulose slows down any moving organism.

(*d*) Place a clean cover-slip on the mixture.

(*e*) Examine the preparation under the microscope, first using the low power, then using high power. Figure 11 should help you to recognise *Paramecium* and *Euglena*. (There may be other organisms present in the cultures as well.)

(*f*) Record your observations as annotated drawings.

Show this work to your tutor.

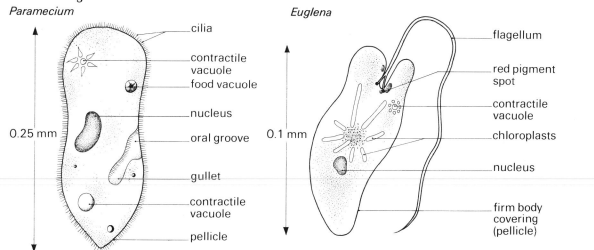

Paramecium — cilia, contractile vacuole, food vacuole, nucleus, oral groove, gullet, contractile vacuole, pellicle, 0.25 mm

Euglena — flagellum, red pigment spot, contractile vacuole, chloroplasts, nucleus, firm body covering (pellicle), 0.1 mm

SWANSEA COLLEGE

3.3 The electron microscope

You can see from figure 9 that the electron microscope is a much more powerful device than the light microscope and can therefore be used for detailed investigation of the structures of cell organelles. The detail revealed by the electron microscope is called the **ultrastructure** of the cell and forms the main content of this section.

A microscope is used for two purposes: to magnify an object and to **resolve** the fine structure of the object.

If you look at a photograph in a newspaper, you will see it is made up of many small dots. Examining such a photograph with a magnifying lens will only make it appear bigger. It will not be possible to see any finer details, since the distance between the dots is fixed and this limits the detail which can be seen. The resolving power of a microscope refers to the distance between two dots or objects which the microscope can just distinguish as separate.

An object which appears under the light microscope as a dot, when viewed under the electron microscope, will be seen to be larger, due to the greater magnification possible with the electron microscope. But, more importantly, it may be seen to be composed of substructures itself, due to the greater resolving power of the electron microscope.

The resolving power of a microscope depends on a number of factors which include the numerical aperture of the lens, the angle at which the light enters the lens and, most importantly, the wavelength (the distance between the peak of one wave and the next) of the light itself. It is this last factor that is the most important because the shorter the wavelength of the radiation used to produce the image of the object, the greater will be the resolving power of the microscope. An average wavelength of visible light is about 550 nm but the average wavelength of an electron beam is 0.005 nm. A good light microscope can resolve two points 2 μm apart while an electron microscope can resolve objects that are only 1 nm apart.

SAQ 8 Explain what is meant by the term (*a*) wavelength;   (*b*) resolving power.

Figure 12 is a diagram which shows the internal layout of an electron microscope.

The filament of the electron gun at the top end of the electron microscope is heated causing it to emit electrons. These negatively charged electrons are attracted towards the positively charged anode. As they travel towards the anode they accelerate and, at the same time, are concentrated into a narrow beam by the negatively charged cathode. By the time the electrons reach the anode they are moving fast enough to pass through a hole in the anode and 'escape' into the lower part of the electron microscope.

12 The design of an electron microscope

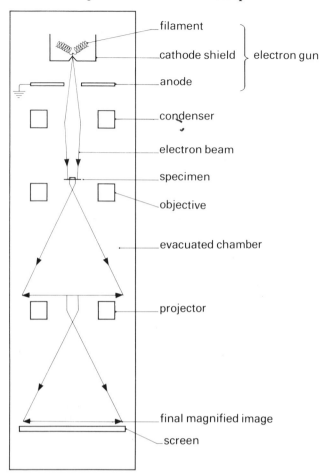

- filament
- cathode shield — electron gun
- anode
- condenser
- electron beam
- specimen
- objective
- evacuated chamber
- projector
- final magnified image
- screen

The beam of electrons now acts in a similar manner to a beam of light as it passes through a condenser, the specimen under investigation and the objective of the electron microscope. The condenser and objective are electromagnets which have the same function in the electron microscope as the corresponding glass lenses in the light microscope.

The projector focuses an image of the specimen onto a screen or micrograph film, thus acting as an eyepiece. Images cannot be viewed directly by eye in the electron microscope because the wavelength of the electron beam is too small.

The whole apparatus is assembled inside an evacuated chamber, otherwise the electron beam would be stopped by collision with air molecules. This means that the specimen must be inserted into the microscope via an air-lock which maintains the vacuum inside the chamber.

SAQ 9 (*a*) What are the functions of (i) a condenser, (ii) an objective?
(*b*) What disadvantage is there in having to use an evacuated chamber with biological material?

The ultrastructure of a young plant cell is revealed in electron micrograph 13. The structures in figure 14 are an interpretation of this micrograph.

13 Electron micrograph of a young plant cell (× 3200)

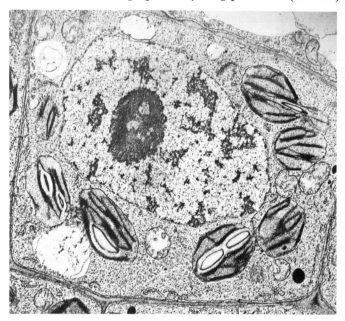

14 Drawing of electron micrograph 13 – a young plant cell

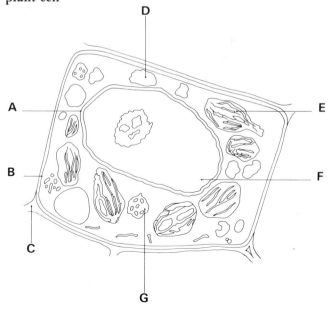

SAQ 10 The structures labelled **A–G** in figure 14 have been listed in objective (*a*) of this section. Identify as many as possible.

You can see in the electron micrograph that those organelles barely visible using the light microscope have a complex structure revealed by the electron microscope.

The drawing of the young plant cell in figure 14 raises the question of interpretation of electron micrographs. If you compare electron micrograph 13 and figure 14 carefully, it will become apparent that the drawing is not a precise copy of the electron micrograph. The micrograph has been interpreted, and this process involves use of previous knowledge of the structures observed and imagination of what is represented by the micrograph. For example, the cell membrane appears to be broken at various points but is drawn as continuous. This is because it is believed to be continuous and any breaks in the micrograph are due to damage caused in preparing the material for electron microscopy or problems in printing the micrograph. You will have the opportunity of developing your own skills of interpretation later in this section but be careful that you only draw what is justified by the knowledge you have and the information available, not simply what you want to see.

SAQ 11 Compare figure 14 with figure 3. Which structure is not present in figure 14 but appears in the plant cells shown in figure 3?

Figure 15 is an electron micrograph of an animal cell. This reveals that the cytoplasm is full of darkly staining areas and membrane-like structures. It is commonly believed that in the cytoplasm of all cells there is a complex membrane system which forms a network throughout the cell called the **endoplasmic reticulum**.

SAQ 12 (*a*) Draw and label the animal cell shown in electron micrograph 15.
(*b*) Compare electron micrographs 13 and 15. Which structures appear in plant cells but not in animal cells and vice versa?
(*c*) Calculate the true size of the nucleus in electron micrograph 13 by measuring its apparent size and using the magnification given.

15 Electron micrograph of an animal cell

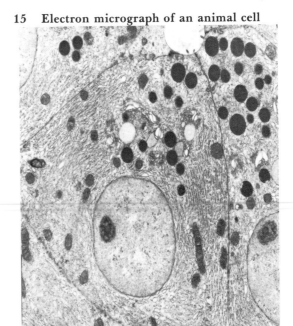

3.4 The detailed ultrastructure and function of the cell

Electron micrograph 13 shows an enlargement of 3200 times. Even more detail can be seen using higher magnifications, and in electron microscopes an enlargement of 500 000 times is possible.

In the remainder of this section you will study the detailed ultrastructure of the cell and also learn something of the function of the various components of the cell.

Figure 16 is a diagram of a generalised animal cell showing the ultrastructure. It is important to note when studying this diagram that no cell has all of these structures, though most cells contain many of them, and also that the endoplasmic reticulum is much more extensive than is shown here. You should refer back to this diagram as you work through the rest of this section so as to keep the various structures in perspective.

3.4.1 The structure concerned with control and heredity

The **nucleus** is the structure concerned with control

16 A generalised animal cell showing ultrastructure

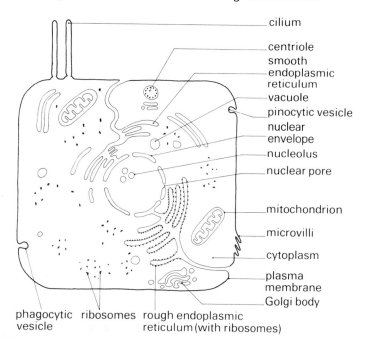

- cilium
- centriole
- smooth endoplasmic reticulum
- vacuole
- pinocytic vesicle
- nuclear envelope
- nucleolus
- nuclear pore
- mitochondrion
- microvilli
- cytoplasm
- plasma membrane
- Golgi body

phagocytic vesicle   ribosomes   rough endoplasmic reticulum (with ribosomes)

of the metabolic activities of a cell and the inheritance of characteristics from generation to generation of cells and organisms.

There is usually one nucleus per cell. It is generally spherical or egg-shaped and has its longest dimension varying between 5–20 μm.

17   Electron micrograph of a cell nucleus

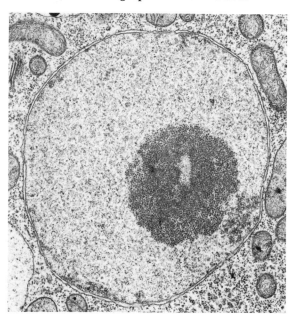

SAQ 13 Would a cell nucleus be visible using a light microscope?

Electron micrograph 17 of a nucleus reveals a densely staining region called the **nucleolus** embedded in the nucleoplasm. The nucleoplasm is a semi-fluid material which also contains fibres of chromatin and is bounded by two membranes forming the **nuclear envelope.**

The nucleus shown in electron micrograph 17 is a non-dividing one. During nuclear division, chromosomes become visible within the nucleus, as in figure 18.

18   Chromosomes in the nucleus of a dividing cell

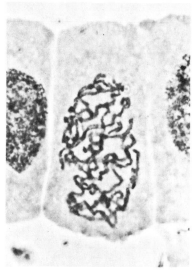

Although **chromosomes** cannot be recognised in a non-dividing nucleus, they are present as very elongated, thin structures. These take up stain at various points along their length and do not, therefore, appear as continuous structures.

SAQ 14 Which structures in the non-dividing cell represent chromosomes?

During division, these elongated chromatin fibres coil up, so becoming visible. The chromosomes contain DNA molecules and it is these which carry the instructions for the production of proteins which control all the cell's metabolic activities.

The DNA molecule is also capable of producing exact copies of itself so that every time a nucleus divides each new nucleus has a precise copy of the instructions for protein production. This information is passed on from generation to generation during cell reproduction and ensures that each new cell can develop in the same way as the mother cell. DNA is therefore regarded as the hereditary material.

SAQ 15 What is meant by hereditary material?

The nucleolus is indirectly involved in the cell's control mechanism because it produces ribosomes which are involved in protein production in the cytoplasm.

The nuclear envelope is two membranes with openings, called nuclear pores, over its surface. It generally acts as a barrier between the nucleoplasm and cytoplasm, and probably has a protective function with regard to the thin elongated chromosomes. The nuclear pores provide a connecting link for any necessary exchange of materials between the nucleus and cytoplasm.

SAQ 16 From the information given above, suggest two materials which must pass across the nuclear envelope.

At this point is it worth pausing to consider the three-dimensional nature of the structures represented by the two-dimensional figures and electron micrographs in this section. For example, the nuclear envelope appears as a flat circular structure in electron micrograph 17 when in reality it is spherical. You should always try to imagine the three-dimensional structure of the various organelles described in this section and, if possible, examine a suitable model showing cell ultrastructure.

3.4.2 Structures which act as barriers at cell surfaces

The cell membrane is a single membrane, often called a **plasma membrane**, and is found in all cells. Apart from holding the cell contents together, it also has the function of regulating the passage of materials into and out of the cell.

SAQ 17 What general difference, if any, is there in structure and function between the cell membrane and the nuclear envelope?

In cells concerned with absorption, secretion or excretion, for example those lining the mammalian small intestine and kidney tubules, the plasma membrane is extended to form structures called **microvilli**, as shown in electron micrograph 19.

19   Electron micrograph of microvilli

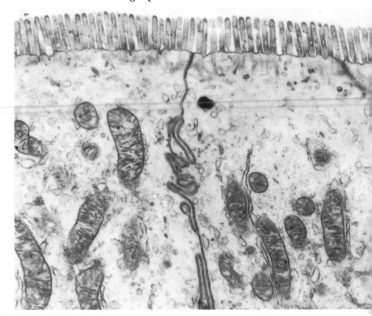

SAQ 18 What advantage is gained by having such a folded cell membrane?

In plant cells a **cell wall** is laid down on the cell membrane as shown in electron micrograph 20. This is generally referred to as the cellulose cell wall because it largely consists of cellulose and hemicellulose. The cellulose cell wall does not function as a barrier but as a supporting structure. At some stage all plant cells have a thin, transparent primary cell wall less than 1 μm thick which, whilst being strong and inelastic, is a non-rigid structure. Some plant cells have, in addition to this primary cell wall, a secondary cell wall which is laid down between the primary one and the cell membrane. The secondary cell wall is usually 10–50 μm thick and quite rigid. Walls of adjacent cells are cemented together by a thin layer called the **middle lamella**.

SAQ 19 What are the major differences between primary and secondary cell walls?

Although cellulose cell walls do not usually function as barriers, they can do so if they become impregnated with waxy materials to form a cuticle that is

20   Electron micrograph of a plant cell wall

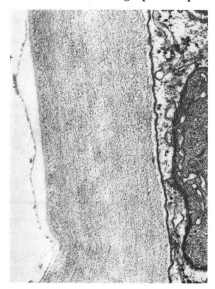

impermeable to water. Such a conversion occurs in the surface layers of certain plants and prevents excessive evaporation from the plant.

3.4.3 Structures which connect cells

Fine strands of cytoplasm link up neighbouring cells in both plants and animals. In plant cells strands pass through fine channels in the cellulose cell walls and middle lamella, and are known as **plasmodesmata** (see figure 21).

21   Electron micrograph of plasmodesmata (× 3600)

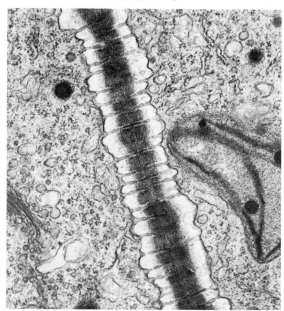

In animal cells, the neighbouring plasma membranes are generally 20–30 nm apart but may be joined by structures called **desmosomes**. Desmosomes are modifications of the cell membranes of two neighbouring cells in a particular region which have strands of cytoplasm running through them. Both plasmodesmata and desmosomes are probably involved in movement of materials between cells, although desmosomes also appear to have a mechanical supporting function in animal cells.

SAQ 20 How far apart are the plant cell membranes shown in electron micrograph 21?

3.4.4 Structures concerned with movement

Cilia, flagella, basal bodies and centrioles are all structures concerned with movement. They are based on arrangements of contractile protein fibres called microtubules.

Cilia are usually present in large numbers on the outside of certain types of cell.

They may be concerned with locomotion in organisms such as *Paramecium* but also perform other functions; for example, those on the outer cells of the human respiratory tract move mucus over the surface.

They are usually between 5–10 μm in length and have an outer membrane which is a continuation of the cell membrane. This encloses an outer ring of paired microtubules surrounding a central pair as shown in electron micrographs 22 and 23.

22   Electron micrograph of cilia (LS – longitudinal section)

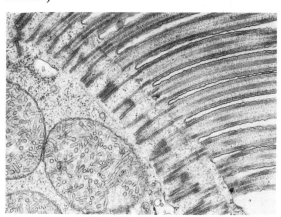

23 Electron micrograph of cilia (TS – transverse section)

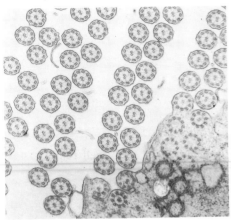

SAQ 21 (*a*) Which microtubules in electron micrograph 22 appear to originate in the basal bodies?
(*b*) How many outer pairs of microtubules are found in cilia, from the information in electron micrograph 22?
(*c*) How many microtubules are there in a basal body?

Flagella are hair-like structures found on the outside of cells (as in electron micrograph 24) which may be up to $150 \, \mu$m long.

24 Electron micrograph of a euglenoid organism showing flagella (× 1000)

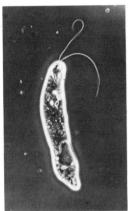

Flagella may act as organs of locomotion in certain organisms such as *Euglena*. Movement of the organism is caused by the action of the flagella against the surrounding fluid medium. They have the same arrangement of microtubules, called 'the 9 + 2 arrangement', as do cilia, and also originate in a basal body.

SAQ 22 How many microtubules are found in a cilium or flagellum?

In all animal cells, and some plant cells, structures called **centrosomes** can be found. They are areas of differentiated cytoplasm involved in the production of spindle fibres and the movement of chromosomes during nuclear division (see figure 25).

25 Movement of chromosomes

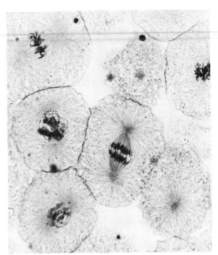

The centrosome contains a pair of **centrioles** arranged at right-angles to each other. Centrioles are similar in structure to the basal bodies of cilia and flagella, but they have a 9 × 3 arrangement of microtubules (see figure 26).

26 Electron micrograph of a centrosome showing arrangement of centrioles and microtubules

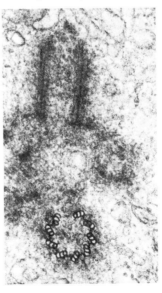

SAQ 23 List three differences between basal bodies and centrioles.

3.4.5 Structures concerned with synthesis

The endoplasmic reticulum (ER) consists of membrane-bound cavities which appear throughout the cytoplasm and may, in certain parts, be continuous with the nuclear and cell membranes. Three types of ER are usually distinguishable in electron micrographs, smooth ER, rough ER and the Golgi body (often called a dictyosome in plant cells).

Smooth ER (electron micrograph 27) has flattened cavities and is believed to be involved in the manufacture of lipids and steroids. **Rough ER** (electron micrograph 28) has tubular parallel cavities with ribosomes attached to the outer surface. The ribosomes, which are also found free in the cytoplasm, are the sites of protein synthesis, and the rough ER is believed to be involved with isolating and secreting those proteins, such as hormones and digestive enzymes, which have extracellular functions. The **Golgi body** (electron micrograph 29) is similar in structure to smooth ER except that it is closely associated with vesicles which sometimes contain granules. It may be involved in the secretion of glycoproteins, often enzyme molecules wrapped in an inactivating carbohydrate coat. The Golgi body may also be responsible for cell wall and cell membrane production. The products of both rough ER and the Golgi body are believed to pass out of the cell by being moved along the inside of the cavities to the outer membrane. They are thus kept isolated and cannot affect the cell's metabolism.

SAQ 24 State one difference between smooth ER and rough ER and one similarity between smooth ER and the Golgi body.

Ribosomes are amongst the smallest structures found in the cytoplasm and were only discovered with the advent of the electron microscope. They are composed of RNA and protein and are the most numerous structures in the cell.

SAQ 25 Where do ribosomes originate in the cell?

27 Electron micrograph of smooth endoplasmic reticulum

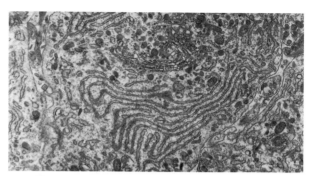

28 Electron micrograph of rough endoplasmic reticulum

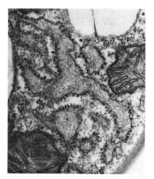

29 Electron micrograph of a Golgi body

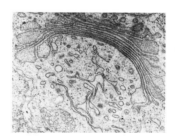

3.4.6 Structures involved in carbohydrate metabolism

Chloroplasts are found in the green cells of plants and are lens-shaped structures 5–15 μm long and 2–5 μm wide (see figure 30).

The outer wall is a double membrane (envelope) which separates the chloroplast from the cytoplasm and encloses a series of flattened structures called **lamellae**. The lamellae are composed of two membranes, one on top of the other. Sometimes, these form sac-like structures which are called

30 A three-dimensional interpretation of chloroplast structure

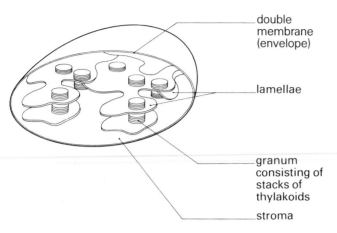

double membrane (envelope)

lamellae

granum consisting of stacks of thylakoids

stroma

thylakoids. These are embedded in a proteinaceous fluid called the **stroma.** The lamellae, which are arranged in stacks, or **grana,** at various points, contain the green pigment chlorophyll and various enzymes involved in the energy-trapping phase of photosynthesis, the process in which green plants produce food using light energy. The stroma contains the ribosomes and enzymes involved in the carbo-hydrate-producing phase of photosynthesis.

31 Electron micrograph of a chloroplast

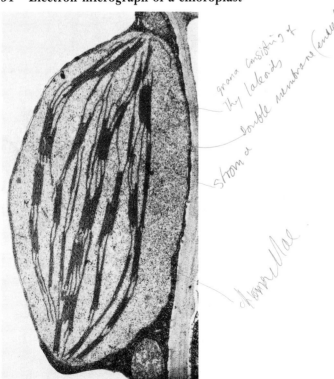

grana consisting of thylakoids

double membrane (envelope)

stroma

chlorophyll

SAQ 26 Draw the chloroplast shown in electron micrograph 31 and label it, using the information given in the text and diagram 30.

Mitochondria are found in the cytoplasm of both animal and plant cells. They are spherical or rod-shaped structures $1.5-10.0\,\mu m$ long and $0.5-3.0\,\mu m$ wide. A mitochondrion is separated from the cyto-plasm by an outer membrane which encloses an inner membrane. Inside the inner membrane is a fluid-filled space called the matrix (see figure 32).

32 Three-dimensional interpretations of mitochondrial structure

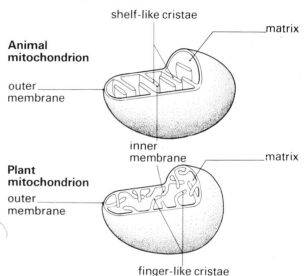

shelf-like cristae

matrix

Animal mitochondrion

outer membrane

inner membrane

matrix

Plant mitochondrion

outer membrane

finger-like cristae

The inner membrane is folded into structures called cristae. These may be finger-like in plant cells and shelf-like in animal cells, but both forms may occur in animals or plants. Mitochondria contain enzymes which help in the breakdown of carbohydrates and release of energy for the cell's activities. The number of mitochondria in a cell can vary from just a few in relatively inactive cells to many thousands in very active cells.

SAQ 27 (a) Draw one mitochondrion from electron micrograph 33 and label it using the information given in the text and figure 32.
(b) Why is there apparently a relationship between the activity of a cell and the number of mitochondria it contains?
(c) List three similarities and three differences between mitochondria and chloroplasts.

33 Electron micrograph of mitochondria

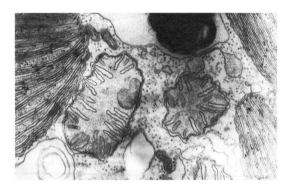

3.4.7 Vesicles and vacuoles

Vesicles and vacuoles are membrane-lined structures found in the cytoplasm.

Pinocytic vesicles are formed as a result of the cell membrane folding into the cell and then closing off, having trapped small particles and any surrounding fluid.

Phagocytic vesicles are formed when a cell engulfs food particles by flowing around them. This happens in unicellular organisms such as *Amoeba* and cells such as white blood cells in mammals (see figure 34).

34   Phagocytosis

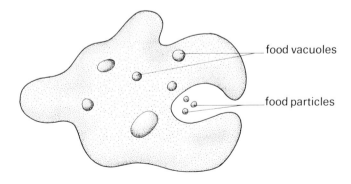

food vacuoles

food particles

These vesicles enable liquids or solids to be brought into the cell and their contents to be ultimately assimilated or egested.

SAQ 28 What would have to happen to the pinocytic and phagocytic vesicles before their contents become available to the cell?

Lysosomes are cell vesicles which are believed to contain enzymes capable of digesting cell components and proteins. They originate in the Golgi body and will digest the cell contents if broken open. Normally they are released only at cell death, although it is thought they may sometimes be used in breaking down worn-out organelles and cytoplasmic proteins. Lysosomes have only been observed in animal cells.

SAQ 29 What possible advantage is there to a cell in having such potentially dangerous vesicles as lysosomes around?

Plant cell central vacuoles are characteristic of plant cells but vary considerably in size and may not always be apparent in young cells. They contain a solution of mineral salts and sugars called the cell sap and, in mature cells, the vacuole can occupy almost the whole cell (see electron micrograph 35). The

35   Electron micrograph of a mature plant cell showing the central vacuole

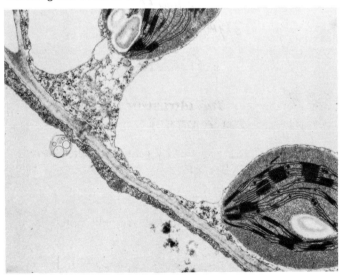

vacuole plays a major role in maintaining the shape and form of the plant cell by means of the pressure developed by the fluid contents. This vacuole is surrounded by a membrane known as the **tonoplast**.

SAQ 30 Draw the above plant cell and label it using the information contained previously in this section.

Contractile vacuoles are water-containing sacs which function as pumps in fresh-water unicellular organisms such as *Amoeba* and *Paramecium*. They are used to collect excess water which diffuses into the cell. Eventually they discharge this water back into the surroundings through a small pore in the cell membrane (see figure 36).

36 *Paramecium* **showing contractile vacuole**

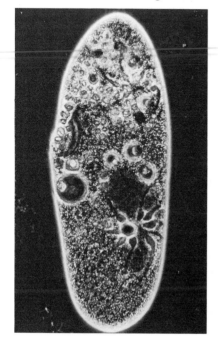

3.5 Extension: The ultrastructure and function of the living cell

Reference: *The Living Cell* by Jean Brachet, *Scientific American*, September 1961.

Answer the following questions.

1 Which 'functional capacities' are cells noted as having in common?

2 List the kinds of light microscopy used to photograph the same three *Paramecium*. What appears to be the advantages of these different kinds?

3 Which of the characteristics of living organisms are not displayed by viruses?

4 Which cytoplasmic organelles have the 'property of self-replication'? When is this property observed?

5 What are the endoplasmic reticulum functions mentioned in the article?

6 What advantage is suggested in the diffuse distribution of chromatin in the nucleus?

7 Summarise 'the role of the nucleus in the economy of the cell'.

Show this work to your tutor.

3.6 Summary assignment 3

1 Copy out and complete table 37 on page 20.

2 The diagram drawn in SAQ 12 should be included with your summary notes. List underneath the diagram the structures that are present in plant cells but absent in animal cells.

Show this work to your tutor.

3.7 Past examination questions

The following questions are taken from past A-level examination papers. Answers to these should be handed in to your tutor. The diagram for question 2 should be copied; it will be a useful summary of cell ultrastructure.

1 Write concise notes on **each** of the following.
(*a*) mitochondria
(*b*) nucleoli
(*c*) endoplasmic reticulum
How has electron microscopy changed our views on the structure of cells?

2 Figure 38 illustrates a section through a plant cell as seen with the aid of an electron microscope.
(*a*) Identify the parts labelled **1–16**.
(*b*) Briefly explain the parts played by structures **5, 6** and **13** in the metabolism of the plant.
(*c*) Give **three** differences, which would be seen by electron microscopy, between an animal cell, such as an absorptive cell, and a plant cell like the one in the diagram.

Show this work to your tutor.

Self test 3, page 83, covers section 3 of this unit.

37 Table for summary assignment 3

Region	Structure	General function	Specific function
nucleus	nucleolus	control	————————
	chromosome		————————
	nuclear envelope		————————
surface	cell membrane	barriers	————————
	cuticle		————————
	plasmodesmata	connections	————————
	desmosomes		————————
	cilia		————————
	flagella	movement	————————
cytoplasm	basal body		————————
	centriole		————————
	ribosomes	protein synthesis	————————
	Golgi body		————————
	smooth ER	secretion	————————
	rough ER		————————
	chloroplasts	carbohydrate	————————
	mitochondrion	metabolism	————————
	pinocytic vesicles		————————
	phagocytic vesicles		————————
	plant cell vacuoles	various	————————
	contractile vacuoles		————————

38 Figure for question 2

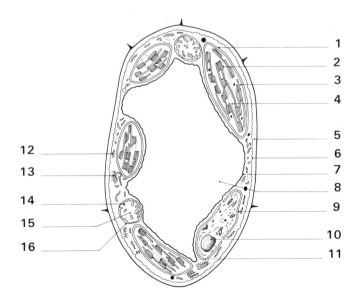

Section 4 Chemical evolution

4.1 Introduction and objectives

The cells of all living organisms are very similar in their general structure, chemistry and organisation. This fact can easily be overlooked because the differences between cells tend to be emphasised and the underlying similarities ignored. It is also true that all new cells originate from other cells. The implication which has been drawn from these facts is that life originated in the form of a cell-like structure and that all living organisms have evolved from the original cell or similar ones formed at about the same time.

The first steps in the origin of life are believed to have involved the formation of a 'pre-cell' from certain chemicals available in the early history of the Earth. A pre-cell is simply a structure which, although it would not satisfy modern cell theory, bears certain resemblances to a cell and can be recognised as a possible ancestor. In this section you will consider how such a pre-cell could have been formed by a process called chemical evolution in the conditions existing at the origin of life.

After completing this section you should be able to do the following.

(a) Describe the conditions in which life may have originated.

(b) Outline a possible pathway for the chemical evolution of a pre-cell.

Extension

(a) Discuss the development of cell theory and ideas about the origin of life from 1600 to the present day and, in particular, the influence of technological advances on this theory.

4.2 Conditions at the origin of life

4.2.1 The origin and age of the Earth

The most widely supported hypothesis about the origin of the solar system suggests that it began as a vast revolving cloud of gas in space.

Gravitational forces caused contraction of this cloud which raised the temperature of its central mass until thermonuclear reactions set in and a new star, the sun, was formed. This was surrounded by a belt of gas and dust from which the planets were formed by local eddies (figure 39).

39 **Formation of the sun and planets**

The sun and its associated planets constitute our solar system with all the planets orbiting the sun in the same direction and plane, having formed at the same time. The evidence available from dating of meteorites (4550 million years), moon rock (4600 million years) and the oldest Earth rock (4550 million years) indicates an approximate age of 5000 million years for our solar system (figure 40).

4.2.2 The chemical composition of the early Earth

The Earth began as a mass of gas and dust made up of various elements, including oxygen, hydrogen,

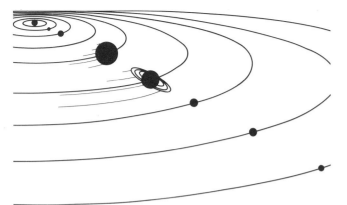

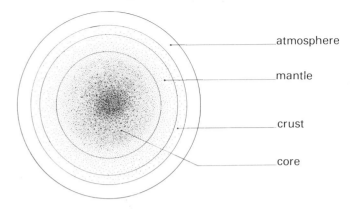

carbon, nitrogen, silicon, iron, nickel and aluminium. As this mass condensed, the heavier substances sank while the lighter ones formed an atmosphere from which the oxygen and hydrogen gradually escaped (figure 41).

41 Chemical composition of the early Earth

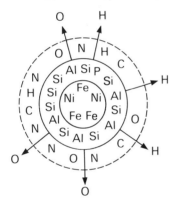

As the condensing mass cooled, compounds began to form. This occurred especially in the cooler atmospheric layer. Here the carbon, hydrogen, oxygen and nitrogen present formed methane (CH_4), ammonia (NH_3), cyanogen (C_2N_2), steam (H_2O) and carbon dioxide (CO_2). Some hydrogen remained in the free state. The inner layer, called the mantle, consisted of molten rock, composed of compounds of silicon, aluminium, iron etc. As cooling continued, a thin crust of solid rock was formed on top of the liquid mantle. The central core was molten material, mainly iron and nickel (figure 42).

Some scientists believe that a new atmosphere was formed by gases escaping through the thin crust

which was continually broken by the molten mantle. Such gases would have been reduced ones such as methane and ammonia. However, other scientists believe that the atmosphere was formed from oxidised gases such as steam and carbon dioxide which collected during the last stages of condensation. Scientists agree that a very important point is that **all** gaseous oxygen escaped from the atmosphere.

4.2.3 Physical conditions

As the Earth cooled further, the water in the atmosphere condensed and torrential rain fell for thousands of years forming vast rivers which carried dissolved minerals from the crust into the oceans. Violent electrical storms must have occurred frequently and, as the oxygen content of the atmosphere decreased to nothing, more and more ultraviolet radiation could penetrate from the sun to the Earth's surface (figure 43).

43 Physical conditions on early Earth

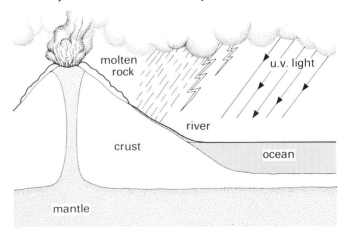

SAQ 31 Summarise the conditions which existed (*a*) in the atmosphere, (*b*) in the oceans, and (*c*) in terms of possible energy sources, at the time life is believed to have originated.

4.3 The theory of chemical evolution

During the first few decades of this century, a number of scientists, notably the Russian A. I. Oparin and J. B. S. Haldane in Britain, suggested that, given these chemical and physical conditions, a process of chemical evolution could have occurred. It was suggested that a variety of simple organic molecules could have been produced by chemical reactions in the oceans, fuelled by the various energy sources. The products of these reactions gradually accumulated in the oceans, forming what Haldane referred to as a 'primeval soup'.

Once amino acids, fatty acids and simple carbohydrates had accumulated in sufficient concentrations, polymerisation to form lipids, proteins and larger carbohydrates could have occurred.

SAQ 32 Why was the absence of gaseous oxygen important at this stage of chemical evolution?

These compounds would have formed a rich soup of materials in the warm oceans, from which a cell could be built. In the 1950s this hypothesis of chemical evolution received experimental support.

4.3.1 Experimental evidence for chemical evolution

In 1953, Stanley Miller and Harold Urey, then at the University of Chicago, carried out an experiment to test the hypothesis put forward by Oparin and Haldane that chemical evolution could have occurred in the conditions which existed on early Earth. Using the apparatus shown in figure 44, they recreated the probable conditions of the primitive Earth in the reaction chamber of their apparatus.

SAQ 33 Examine the diagram of Miller's and Urey's apparatus in figure 44.
(*a*) A vacuum pump was used to evacuate the apparatus before the hydrogen, methane and

44   Miller and Urey's apparatus

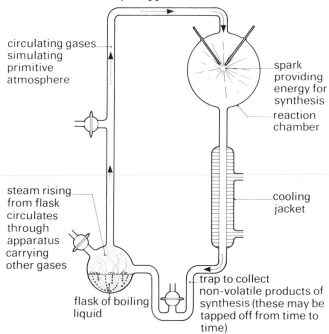

ammonia was allowed in. Why was this done?
(*b*) What is the function of the boiling water and cooling jacket?
(*c*) What energy source is used for the reaction chamber?
(*d*) How do the conditions in the reaction chamber compare with those believed to have existed before the evolution of life?

The accumulated products of the reactions were analysed and found to contain a mixture of 15 amino acids, fatty acids and other simple organic molecules.

Miller's experiment is probably the best known, but other investigations also lend weight to the chemical evolution theory. In 1951, Melvin Calvin at the University of California, Berkeley, irradiated a mixture of carbon dioxide and water with gamma rays and found that appreciable quantities of formic acid (methanoic acid) and formaldehyde (methanal) were produced. Later, using the same starting ingredients as Miller, he was able to produce 6-carbon sugars, amino acids and purines and pyrimidines by irradiation.

More recently, Sidney Fox at the University of Miami has been able to take the amino acids which can be synthesised from a primitive atmosphere, apply heat under dry conditions and produce protein-like polypeptides. Nucleic acids have been produced simply by heating together nucleotides under pressure.

SAQ 34 (*a*) Which four of the chemicals synthesised in the experiments described are regarded as the basic chemicals of life?
(*b*) How do these experimental results support the theory of chemical evolution?

Experiments show that it is possible to produce the kinds of molecules which we know are typical of life today. It will be apparent to you that there is an enormous jump in complexity from a soup of molecules to the highly organised structures known as cells.

4.3.2 Increase in the complexity of molecules

Over vast periods of time, it is possible that, through chemical reactions, smaller molecules were linked together and the organic compounds became increasingly complex and diverse. For this polymerisation to occur, the simpler molecules must have become sufficiently concentrated. This could have occurred in several different ways.

(*a*) By adsorption onto the surface of mineral particles, perhaps after being blown by the wind on the surface layer of oceans and being concentrated in the form of breaking waves (figure 45).

46 Developments in technology, cell theory and ideas concerning the origin of life

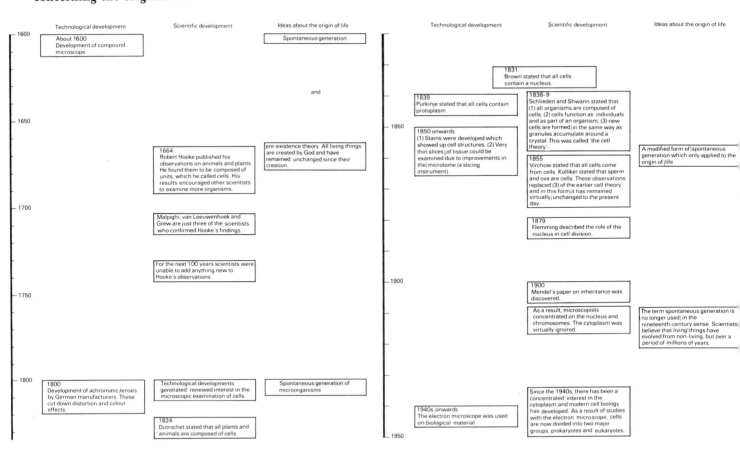

45 Mineral particle with adsorbed molecules

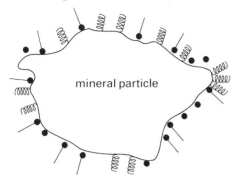

mineral particle

(*b*) It has been shown that polymerisation can occur in dilute solutions of amino acids in the presence of cyanogen derivatives and ultraviolet radiation. Conditions such as these were present in Miller and Urey's experiments.

(*c*) Amino acids have been made to form polymers at high temperatures and pressures such as occur naturally in lavas and volcanic ash.

SAQ 35 What important biological molecules are comprised of the following smaller molecules: amino acids, fatty acids, sugars and nucleotides?

With the passage of time, therefore, complex organic molecules could have appeared in the 'soup' and protein molecules may have played an important role in the next stage of chemical evolution.

Protein molecules are polar and therefore tend to be attracted to each other and form aggregates. Water molecules are also polar and when attracted to protein aggregates form an organised layer around them. Sometimes these aggregates may separate from the main body of a liquid as a kind of particle. These particles are called colloidal particles, and although small enough to pass through some filter papers they are much larger than normal solute molecules of a similar solution. Colloids may be regarded as being midway between a solution and a suspension.

When individual protein–water aggregates approach each other, the outer layer of water molecules may coalesce to form a larger association of protein–water particles. Because the water does not exist in a free association of molecules but in a more definite 'bound' structural state, a sharp boundary can be seen between the particles and the remaining water.

This separation of colloidal particles is known as **coacervation** and the colloid portion is known as a **coacervate** (see figure 47).

47 Coacervate formation

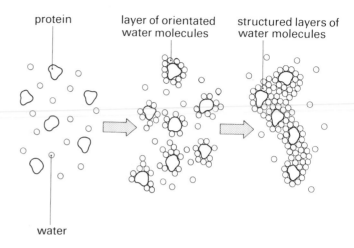

protein

layer of orientated water molecules

structured layers of water molecules

water

SAQ 36 How would the formation of coacervates aid chemical evolution?

There is clearly a large gap between a coacervate and even the simplest of living organisms.

The next three sections in this unit will discuss how this gap might have been bridged with respect to three of the most important aspects of cellular structure and function. These are the cell's energy relationships, barrier systems and control mechanisms.

4.4 Summary assignment 4

List in sequence the steps which would lead from a primitive atmosphere to the formation of a pre-cell. Show this work to your tutor..

4.5 Extension: The development of the cell theory

The history of the development of cell theory is an interesting example of how science progresses. It illustrates how an important conceptual development was postponed by an underdeveloped technology and contemporary ideas about the origin of life. The sequence of events is shown in table 46.

SAQ 37 (*a*) For what reasons did the development of the cell theory span a period of about 200 years?
(*b*) How did the original Schleiden/Schwann cell theory differ from the one that is accepted today?
(*c*) What technological development of this century has expanded our knowledge of the cell?

AV 4: Spontaneous generation and the origin of life

Materials

VCR and monitor
ABAL video sequence: *Spontaneous generation*
Worksheets: 8, 9 and 10

Procedure

(*a*) Check that you have all the relevant materials listed above.

(*b*) Check that the video cassette is set up ready to show the appropriate sequence – *Spontaneous generation*.

(*c*) Start the sequence and either stop it at the appropriate point to complete worksheets 8, 9 and 10 as you go, or complete the worksheets at the end of the sequence.

(*d*) If you do not understand anything, then stop the sequence, rewind and study the relevant material again before consulting with your tutor.

(*e*) If possible, work through the sequence and worksheets with a small group and discuss the material with them.

Section 5 Cells and energy

5.1 Introduction and objectives

One of the most obvious characteristics of living cells is their activity. Cells are constantly involved in exchanging materials with their environment and moving chemicals to and from various sites in the cell where they are involved in metabolic reactions.

All of the activities of a cell require energy which is provided from chemical reactions. In this section the nature of energy and its role in cells will be revealed. The significance of energy availability and use in the formation of cells at the origin of life will be discussed.

After completing this section you should be able to do the following.

(a) Define the term energy and state its units of measurement.

(b) Define and give examples of the following types and forms of energy:
potential, kinetic, chemical, electrical, mechanical, nuclear, radiant, activation, free.

(c) Explain the boulder analogy, energy conversions and energy barriers.

(d) State the first and second laws of thermo-dynamics.

(e) Explain the energy consequences for living organisms of the laws of thermodynamics.

(f) Explain the following terms with respect to chemical reactions:
exergonic, endergonic, coupling, reduction, oxidation, net energy change.

(g) State the basic formulae of, and describe the overall energy changes involved in, photosynthesis and respiration.

(h) Explain the role of ATP (adenosine triphosphate) and ADP (adenosine diphosphate) in the metabolism of living organisms.

Extension

(a) Describe what is meant by the heterotroph hypothesis.

(b) Describe the techniques involved in tracing atoms in living systems.

5.2 Programmed learning text: Energy and life

For an explanation of how to work through this programmed text, see the section 'How to use this unit' at the front of the book.

1 Energy is usually described as 'the capacity to do work' and is measured in joules (represented by the symbol J). One joule (1 J) is defined as the energy transferred when a force of one newton (1 N) moves a distance of one metre (1 m) in its direction of action.

Q Write an equation which expresses 1 J in terms of the basic SI units of mass (kg), length (m) and time (s). (Remember that $1 N = 1 kg\,m\,s^{-2}$.)

A $1 J = 1 kg\,m^2\,s^{-2}$ (expressed as one kilogram metre squared per second squared)

2 There are two main types of energy, potential and kinetic.

Potential energy is stored energy whereas kinetic energy is active energy, such as the energy of movement. A piece of steak represents potential energy whilst a charging bull represents kinetic energy.

Q Which type of energy is represented by
(a) a boulder rolling down a hill?
(b) sugars stored in a leaf?
(c) a contracting muscle?
(d) a loaf of bread?
(e) a can of petrol?

A (*a*) kinetic (*b*) potential (*c*) kinetic
(*d*) potential (*e*) potential

3 Potential and kinetic energy occur in different energy forms: chemical, electrical, mechanical, nuclear, radiant.

Chemical energy is stored in chemical compounds and may be released when such compounds are broken down.

Electrical energy is the movement of electrons along a conductor.

Mechanical energy is energy involved in moving matter.

Nuclear energy is released when matter is converted into energy.

Radiant energy is energy such as light which travels in waves.

Q Indicate which form(s) of energy is/are represented by
(*a*) an atom bomb exploding.
(*b*) a carbohydrate molecule.
(*c*) a wire connecting a bright light bulb.
(*d*) a windmill.

A (*a*) nuclear, radiant (*b*) chemical
(*c*) electrical, radiant (*d*) mechanical

4 Energy may be converted from one form to another. Two of the examples given in the previous frame involved energy conversions. The nuclear energy released in an atomic explosion is converted into radiant heat and light energy; the electrical energy in a wire conducting an electron flow to a light bulb is converted into radiant light and heat energy. Indeed, all the forms of energy are capable of being converted into any of the other forms.

Q Suggest some examples of energy conversions involving changes of
(*a*) chemical to mechanical energy.
(*b*) mechanical to electrical energy.
(*c*) radiant to chemical energy.

A (*a*) a petrol-driven car (*b*) a hydro-electric generator (*c*) photosynthesis
(You may have suggested other correct answers, of course.)

5 The petrol-driven car is not only an example of a chemical form of energy being converted into a mechanical form but also of potential energy being converted into kinetic energy. Another example of this is illustrated in figure 48.

48   The conversion of potential into kinetic energy

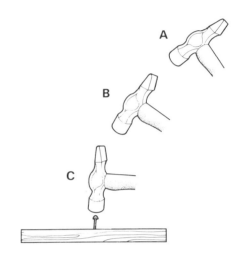

The potential energy of the hammer held at position **A** is converted to kinetic energy as it descends to position **C** over the nail.

Q (*a*) In which position is (i) the potential energy, and (ii) the kinetic energy, at a maximum?
(*b*) What work will be done by the hammer's energy?

A (*a*) (i) position **A** (ii) position **C**
(*b*) The nail will be moved into the object (assuming the hammer hits it!).

6 In thermodynamics, the word system is used to describe the matter which is being referred to. Thus, in frame 3, an atom bomb exploding, a carbohydrate molecule, a wire connecting a bright light bulb, and a windmill were all examples of systems.

Q What system was referred to in figure 48?

A A hammer, nail and object.
In this system energy was transferred from the hammer to the nail and work was done in moving the nail into the object. These changes in the system are referred to as changes of state of the system.

7 When energy conversions occur, no energy is destroyed or lost in the conversion. This is in accordance with the **first law of thermodynamics** which states that energy is neither created nor destroyed but may change forms. However, in each conversion, some of the original energy form will not be converted into the new energy form. This is in accordance with the **second law of thermodynamics** which states that energy conversions are never totally efficient.

The energy which escapes conversion is referred to as useless energy because it is not available in the new form and it often appears in conversions as heat energy.

Q Indicate whether the following statements are true and in accordance with the first or second law of thermodynamics.
(*a*) Energy within the universe is becoming less available to do useful work.
(*b*) It is not possible to convert all of the chemical energy in a glucose molecule into the mechanical energy of contracting muscle fibres.
(*c*) Solar energy may be converted into chemical energy.

A (*a*) true, second law (*b*) true, second law (*c*) true, first law

8 *Summary frame*

Q (1) Define energy.

(2) What units are used to measure energy?

(3) What are the two main types of energy?

(4) Name five different forms of energy.

(5) Give an example of an energy conversion.

(6) State the first law of thermodynamics.

(7) State the second law of thermodynamics.

A (1) Energy is the capacity to do work.

(2) Joules

(3) Potential and kinetic

(4) Chemical, electrical, mechanical, nuclear and radiant

(5) A petrol-driven car in which chemical is converted into mechanical energy.

(6) The first law of thermodynamics states that energy is neither created nor destroyed but may change form.

(7) The second law of thermodynamics states that energy conversions are never totally efficient; in each conversion some energy will be converted into a 'useless' form.

9 Living organisms may exhibit chemical, electrical, mechanical and radiant forms of energy yet of all the sources available from their environment they can only exploit radiant and chemical sources. Indeed, only green plants can exploit radiant energy and all other organisms are totally dependent on chemical sources.

Obviously, living organisms must be capable of energy conversions and, because such conversions will be inefficient, they must produce a proportion of 'useless' energy, usually heat, each time.

Q Why must organisms have
(*a*) a continual supply of energy, and
(*b*) an efficient method of energy excretion?

A (*a*) They must have a continual supply of energy to make up for the constant loss of energy in energy conversions.
(*b*) They must have an efficient mechanism for getting rid of useless energy because if allowed to build up as heat it would cause damage.

10 All living organisms exploit chemical forms of energy. Even the green plants which can exploit radiant sources of energy will convert it into a chemical form before using it to do work.

The energy which is available to do work in a chemical system is called the **free energy**, represented by G. Energy is converted into and from chemical forms during chemical reactions. Such reactions are classified as **exergonic** if they result in a loss of free energy from the system and **endergonic** if they result in a gain of free energy to the system.

Q If a change of free energy is represented by $\triangle G$, will endergonic or exergonic reactions be $-\triangle G$ or $+\triangle G$?

A endergonic $= +\triangle G$;   exergonic $= -\triangle G$

11 The net change in free energy ($\triangle G$) during chemical reactions can be measured, and show whether they are exergonic or endergonic.

Q Indicate for each of the following reactions whether they absorb or release energy and if they are exergonic or endergonic.
(*a*) glucose + phosphate $\rightarrow$ glucose phosphate ($\triangle G$ measured as $+12.6\,\text{kJ}$)
(*b*) ATP $\rightarrow$ ADP + phosphate ($\triangle G$ measured as $-29.3\,\text{kJ}$)

A (*a*) absorbs and is endergonic.
(*b*) releases and is exergonic.

12 Many of the chemical reactions necessary for life are endergonic. An endergonic reaction requires energy which must be taken in by the system before it can proceed. One way of providing such energy is by linking an endergonic with an exergonic reaction in a process called **coupling**. An example of a coupled reaction is:

glucose + ATP $\rightarrow$ glucose phospate + ADP

Q Which two reactions are coupled in the above example?

A glucose + phosphate $\rightarrow$ glucose phosphate
                ATP $\rightarrow$ ADP + phosphate

13 Q Using the information in frames 10 and 11 state whether the coupled reaction is endergonic or exergonic and the amount of energy it releases or absorbs.

A It is exergonic. $12.6\,\text{kJ}$ are absorbed in the formation of glucose phosphate. $29.3\,\text{kJ}$ are evolved in the breakdown of ATP. Therefore there is a net evolution of $(29.3 - 12.6)$ or $16.7\,\text{kJ}$. $\triangle G$ is $-16.7\,\text{kJ}$

14 The energy relationships involved in chemical reactions may be made clearer by making an analogy (comparison) with the energy relationships involved in moving boulders up and down hills. This analogy is referred to as **the boulder analogy**. Consider the example illustrated in figure 49.

49   The boulder analogy

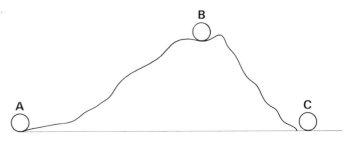

Moving the boulder from position **A** to position **B** would require an investment of energy in the system, whereas the boulder moved from position **B** to position **A** in the system would lose energy as it rolled down the hill.

Q (*a*) Describe the system referred to.
(*b*) Which direction of movement (uphill or downhill) corresponds to (i) endergonic and (ii) exergonic reactions?

A (*a*) The system consists of a boulder and a hill.
(*b*) (i) Uphill is endergonic, (ii) downhill is exergonic.

15 The exergonic reaction in·which the boulder moved from position **B** to position **A** is a spontaneous one. There is nothing to stop the reaction happening and no energy is needed from an outside source. Not all exergonic reactions are spontaneous, however. Consider the boulder moving from position **B** to position **C**. It would have just as much energy as previously but it is prevented from moving by the hump at the top of the hill.

Q What is required to make the boulder move from position **B** to position **C**?

A Sufficient energy to get over the barrier (hump).

16 The energy required to make a reaction start is called activation energy. This is shown in figure 50 where the hill shape is represented on a graph which shows the energy level of molecules and the extent of the reaction.

50   An exergonic reaction pathway

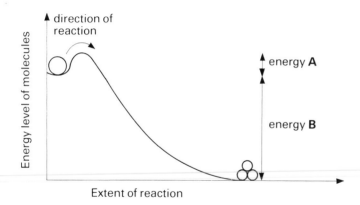

Q Which of the amounts of energy (**A** or **B**) shown in figure 50 corresponds to (*a*) activation energy; (*b*) net energy released, that is free energy, ($-\triangle G$)?

A (*a*) Activation energy is **A**.
(*b*) Net energy released ($-\triangle G$) is **B**.

17 Energy barriers also exist in certain endergonic reactions as illustrated in figure 51.

51   An endergonic reaction pathway

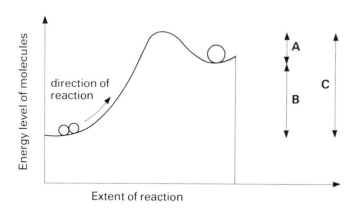

Q (*a*) Which of the amounts of energy **A**, **B** and **C** shown above corresponds to (i) activation energy; (ii) net energy gained; (iii) energy released?
(*b*) Which of these corresponds to the $\triangle G$ for this reaction?

A (*a*) (i) **C** (ii) **B** (iii) **A**
(*b*) **B** = $+\triangle G$ because it is overall an endergonic reaction requiring energy.

18 *Summary frame*

Q (1) Define, and where appropriate, symbolise (*a*) free energy; (*b*) change in free energy; (*c*) endergonic reaction; (*d*) exergonic reaction; (*e*) spontaneous reaction; (*f*) coupled reaction; (*g*) activation energy; (*h*) energy barrier.

(2) Supply labels for figure 52.

52   Reaction pathways

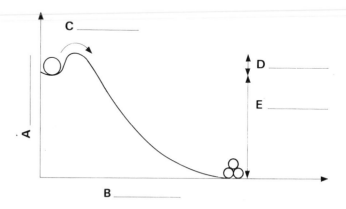

A (1) (*a*) Free energy (*G*) is the energy available to do work in chemical systems.
(*b*) Change in free energy ($\triangle G$) is the amount of energy lost or gained by a system during a reaction.
(*c*) An endergonic reaction is one in which the system gains free energy ($+\triangle G$).
(*d*) An exergonic reaction is one in which the system loses free energy ($-\triangle G$).
(*e*) A spontaneous reaction is one which will happen without an energy input to the system.
(*f*) Coupled reactions are reactions which happen together and involve the loss in free energy of an exergonic reaction begin transferred, in part, to provide the gain in free energy for an endergonic reaction.
(*g*) Activation energy is the energy needed to start a non-spontaneous reaction.
(*h*) Energy barrier is the obstacle, in the boulder analogy, preventing a non-spontaneous reaction starting.

(2) **A** energy level, **B** extent of reaction, **C** direction of reaction, **D** energy barrier or activation energy, **E** change in free energy ($\triangle G$)

19 The ultimate external source of energy for living organisms is the radiant light energy emitted by the sun. Green plants capture this light and convert it into a chemical form in a process called **photosynthesis**.

Photosynthesis involves the conversion of relatively low energy molecules, carbon dioxide and water, into a relatively high energy carbohydrate molecule. The carbohydrate molecule is then directly or indirectly used as a source of energy by all living organisms for their activities.

Q Which of the following applies to the photosynthetic process?
(*a*) exergonic (*b*) endergonic (*c*) increased $\triangle G$
(*d*) decreased $\triangle G$

A (*b*) Endergonic, because it is an energy-capturing process.
(*c*) Increased $\triangle G$, because energy is added to the system from outside.

20 The process in which the energy from carbohydrates is released is called **respiration**. In this process, the carbohydrate interacts with oxygen (is oxidised) and forms carbon dioxide and water whilst releasing energy. The oxidation of glucose can be represented as:

Equation 1

$$C_6H_{12}O_6 + 6O_2 \rightarrow 6CO_2 + 6H_2O + energy$$
glucose   oxygen carbon   water
                       dioxide

Q Which of the following applies to the oxidation of glucose in respiration?
(*a*) exergonic (*b*) endergonic (*c*) increased $\triangle G$
(*d*) decreased $\triangle G$

A (*a*) Exergonic, because it is an energy-releasing process.
(*d*) Decreased $\triangle G$, because energy is lost from the system.

21 The reverse process to oxidation is called reduction (the removal of oxygen or addition of hydrogen to a molecule). The process represented below is a reduction process; carbon dioxide is reduced to glucose.

Equation 2

$$6CO_2 + 6H_2O \rightarrow C_6H_{12}O_6 + 6O_2 + energy$$
carbon   water   glucose   oxygen
dioxide

Q Name the process represented by the above equation.

A Photosynthesis

22 Q which of the following applies to the reduction of carbon dioxide in photosynthesis?
(*a*) exergonic (*b*) endergonic (*c*) increased $\triangle G$
(*d*) decreased $\triangle G$

A (*a*) Endergonic because it takes in energy.
(*b*) Increased $\triangle G$ because energy is gained by the system.

23 Respiration is believed to occur at specific sites in the cell (e.g. in the mitochondria) but the energy released there may be required for chemical reactions occurring elsewhere in the cell.

Somehow, the energy released during respiration must be stored and then released wherever required by the cell.

The agent believed to be responsible for this energy transfer is adenosine triphosphate or ATP. This is a chemical which consists of adenosine (adenine and ribose) linked to three phosphate groups.

Q Which of the following represents ATP
(if $\boxed{A}$ = adenine, $\boxed{R}$ = ribose, $\boxed{P}$ = phosphate)?
(*a*)
$\boxed{A} - \boxed{A} - \boxed{A} - \boxed{R} - \boxed{R} - \boxed{R} - \boxed{P} - \boxed{P} - \boxed{P}$
(*b*) $\boxed{A} - \boxed{R} - \boxed{P}$
(*c*) $\boxed{A} - \boxed{R} - \boxed{R} - \boxed{R} - \boxed{P}$
(*d*) $\boxed{A} - \boxed{R} - \boxed{P} - \boxed{P} - \boxed{P}$

A (*d*) $\boxed{A} - \boxed{R} - \boxed{P} - \boxed{P} - \boxed{P}$

24 During the cellular oxidation of glucose (respiration) ATP is believed to be synthesised from its constituents which are present in the cell.

The equation illustrated below represents the synthesis of ATP, where X is another molecule combined with phosphate (P).

ADP + XP $\longrightarrow$ ATP + X

adenosine   phosphate   adenosine
diphosphate   triphosphate

This synthesis is endergonic. The energy required for it is supplied from that which is released in respiration.

About 40% of the energy released during respiration is transferred from one system (the reacting glucose molecule) to the other (the reacting ADP and P) and becomes 'stored' in ATP. The remaining energy escapes as heat.

Q Write an equation which shows the coupling of ATP production and respiration.

A $C_6H_{12}O_6 + 6O_2 \rightarrow 6CO_2 + 6H_2O$
   $+\ ADP + XP\quad\quad + ATP + X$

25 ATP and ADP are sometimes called the 'high energy' compounds, and the bonds between the two end phosphate groups are sometimes called 'high energy' bonds.

These statements are misleading as energy is not stored in chemical bonds, and when other cellular compounds lose a terminal phosphate group even more energy is released than when ATP is converted to ADP.

However, ATP is believed to be the agent of energy transfer most commonly involved in cellular reactions by a process of energy coupling represented in figure 53.

53   Energy coupling

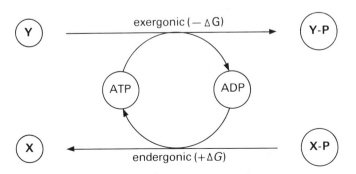

Q Write equations to represent the two reactions which are coupled in figure 53.

A $Y + ATP \rightarrow YP + ADP\ (-\triangle G)$

$XP + ADP \rightarrow X + ATP\ (+\triangle G)$

26 Summary frame

Q (1) Compare and contrast the processes of photosynthesis and respiration by indicating with a P (for photosynthesis) or R (for respiration) which of the following statements is true of either process.
(*a*) A reduction process.
(*b*) An oxidation process.
(*c*) An endergonic process.
(*d*) An exergonic process.
(*e*) A process involving increase $\triangle G$.
(*f*) A process involving decreased $\triangle G$.
(*g*) A process involving the addition of hydrogen to carbon.
(*h*) A process involving the addition of oxygen to carbon.
(*i*) A process involving the removal of oxygen from carbon.
(*j*) A process common to all living organisms.
(*k*) A process restricted to green plants.

(2) Pick examples from the equations given below of reactions which are
(*a*) endergonic, (*b*) exergonic, (*c*) could be coupled, (*d*) involve the synthesis of adenosine triphosphate.
(i) $ADP + XP\quad \rightarrow ATP + X$
(ii) $C_6H_{12}O_6 + 6O_2 \rightarrow 6CO_2 + 6H_2O$
(iii) $Y + ATP\quad\quad \rightarrow YP + ADP$
(iv) $6CO_2 + 6H_2O \rightarrow C_6H_{12}O_6 + 6O_2$

A (1) (*a*) P   (*b*) R   (*c*) P   (*d*) R   (*e*) P   (*f*) R
(*g*) P   (*h*) R   (*i*) P   (*j*) R   (*k*) P

(2) (*a*) (i), (iv)
(*b*) (ii), (iii)
(*c*) (i) + (ii), (i) + (iii), (ii) + (iv), (iii) + (iv)
(*d*) (i), (ii)

5.3 Summary assignment 5

Write down the questions and answers to the review frames of the programmed text 'Energy and life'.

Self test 4, page 84, covers this programmed learning sequence.

5.4 The heterotroph hypothesis - a comprehension exercise

Cellular activities need energy.

In all living cells, the source of this energy is food. One of the most fundamental differences between animals and green plants relates to the method by which they obtain their food. Green plants manufacture their own food from simple inorganic sources. Animals obtain their food from plants, either directly or indirectly. Consider the following hypothesis which could account for this fundamental difference.

In section 4, the process by which molecules such as proteins in the 'primitive soup' could have become grouped as clusters or coacervates is discussed. It is suggested that these gradually evolved into pre-cells or very simple biological systems, which carried out at least some of the activities of living cells. Those activities essential to life (the constant synthesis of proteins, for example) would have been carried out and would have required a continual energy input from the environment. There is no direct evidence about the nature of the pre-cell environment, but it is possible that it harboured several sources of energy. There probably was intense heat (from volcanoes), ultraviolet light (from the sun) and the energy of lightning.

However, this energy would have been released too irregularly to supply the constant energy requirements of pre-cells. Also, intense volcanic heat or lightning would tend to destroy pre-cells rather than maintain them. However, there was one source of energy which was constantly available and safe enough to be used by living systems. The watery environment of pre-cells was probably a 'soup' of organic molecules. Chemical reactions may have occurred between these organic molecules and, in some reactions, energy would be released. It is possible that the ability to take in some of these organic molecules was developed in some pre-cells so

that these chemical reactions occurred inside them. The energy released from the reactions could then supply their needs.

This hypothesis implies that the earliest living organisms obtained organic molecules from their surroundings and used them as energy sources for their activities. These molecules, therefore, represented the food of the pre-cells.

Organisms which obtain food from their surroundings are called **heterotrophs**.

Many biologists believe that the earliest living organisms were heterotrophs. Animals are examples of present-day heterotrophs. This is one way of speculating about the origin of life and is called the heterotroph hypothesis.

The molecules needed by pre-cells for replacement of worn-out parts and for growth and reproduction could also have been taken in from the environment in a similar way. Energy would have been required to build these up into pre-cell materials.

It is possible that the supply of food molecules in the organic 'soup' eventually began to dwindle. Before the supply was exhausted, the ability to make food was developed in some pre-cells. Organisms capable of doing this are called **autotrophs**.

Green plants are examples of some present-day autotrophs in which food (glucose) is made from carbon dioxide and water by a process called photosynthesis. One of the products of photosynthesis is gaseous oxygen, and all the oxygen present in the atmosphere today probably was, and still is, released during photosynthesis.

As the supply of molecules in the 'soup' became exhausted, some heterotrophs may have developed the ability to take in autotrophs in order to obtain food. All present-day heterotrophs obtain food either directly or indirectly from plants.

Autotrophs and heterotrophs differ only in the method by which they obtain food. The mechanism by which all organisms obtain their energy from food is the same and involves harnessing the energy released when food such as glucose undergoes certain chemical reactions in the cell.

Inside cells, food undergoes a series of enzyme-controlled chemical reactions (respiration) during which stored energy is transferred from the food to the cell. As energy can neither be created nor destroyed, it is not 'used up' by the cell but may be returned to the environment as the result of work being done. For example, movement (such as the contraction of a muscle cell) may bring about a temperature increase in the environment of the cell. This can be regarded as a return of energy in the form of heat from the cell to the environment.

Some energy may be redistributed as the stored energy of new cell materials. When cells die and decay, this energy is also eventually returned to the environment.

SAQ 38 (*a*) List some activities for which pre-cells required energy.
(*b*) List the sources of energy available to pre-cells.
(*c*) Which of these sources was most useful to pre-cells, and why?
(*d*) What is (i) a heterotroph, (ii) an autotroph?
(*e*) How do heterotrophs and autotrophs obtain their energy.

5.5 Extension: Methods of studying chemical reactions

Reference: *Understanding the Chemistry of the Cell* by G. R. Barker. Institute of Biology Studies in Biology No. 13.

Chapter 3. Methods of studying chemical reactions of the cell.
The use of isotopic tracers.

Chapter 4. Reactions in cell free systems.
Cell fractionation.
Separating large and small molecules.
Read the above sections and make notes relevant to the following essay question.

'Explain how you would trace the movement of a group of carbon atoms through a unicellular organism.'

Show both your notes and the essay to your tutor.

Section 6 Exchanges between cells and their surroundings

6.1 Introduction and objectives

Cells must control what enters and leaves them in order to survive. They must keep out poisons which would destroy them, and unnecessary molecules which would clutter up the cell and make it inefficient. They must maintain a sufficiently high concentration of certain molecules to ensure the reactions of metabolism. They must get rid of any waste products of metabolism whilst taking in the raw materials needed for growth, repair and energy.

Cells have a barrier called the cell or plasma membrane at the boundary with their external environment. This performs all the above functions and its formation would have been crucial to the survival of the earliest cells. Indeed, so important is such a structure believed to be that it seems likely that the formation of a cell barrier such as the plasma membrane must have been one of the first steps in the evolution of a recognisable cell from the chemical soup.

After completing this section you should be able to do the following.

(a) Describe the chemical nature, structure and dimensions of the plasma membrane according to
(i) Gorter and Grendel's bimolecular lipid layer hypothesis.
(ii) Danielli and Davson's unit membrane model.
(iii) Singer and Nicolson's fluid mosaic model.

(b) Define diffusion and explain which factors may affect the rate of diffusion.

(c) Outline four different ways in which molecules may cross a plasma membrane.

(d) Distinguish between active and passive transport.

(e) Explain what is meant by a partially permeable membrane (PPM) and discuss the significance of such membranes for living organisms.

(f) Define osmosis, water potential, solute potential, pressure potential, haemolysis, turgidity, turgor, hypotonic, hypertonic and isotonic.

(g) Write an equation to represent the water potential of a cell subjected to external pressure.

(h) Given values for the solute and pressure potentials of two systems separated by a PPM, determine whether water will move by osmosis, and if so in which direction.

(i) Explain three mechanisms which animals may employ to overcome problems caused by osmosis and, in particular, explain the action of a contractile vacuole.

(j) Describe how water and solute potentials may be measured in plant tissue.

Extension

(a) Explain the use of the following terms: suction pressure, diffusion pressure deficit, osmotic pressure.

(b) Discuss with reference to the membranes of animal cells:
(i) the range of form and composition;
(ii) methods of cell recognition;
(iii) mechanisms of surface interaction;
(iv) the functioning of the lysosome system.

6.2 The structure of the plasma membrane

The plasma membrane has certain properties which indicate something about the nature of the molecules of which it is composed. Perhaps its most important property is the ability to be selective in allowing certain molecules to pass easily whilst restricting the passage of others. This property is described as partial (or differential) permeability, and it allows the membrane to act as a barrier to 'undesirable'

the same time as a 'gateway' to those molecules necessary for the cell's metabolic activities.

One group of molecules which pass rapidly through the membrane are those which dissolve in lipids.

SAQ 39 What does this property indicate about the structure of the membrane?

Chemical analysis of membranes reveals that lipids are present and one type of lipid, the **phospholipid**, is prevalent. The structure of a phospholipid is shown in figure 54.

54   A phospholipid molecule

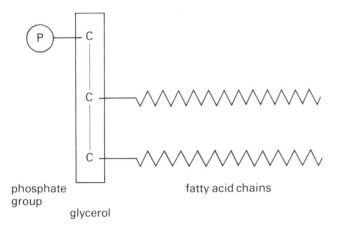

phosphate group

glycerol

fatty acid chains

SAQ 40 How does the phospholipid shown in figure 54 differ from a triglyceride?

Phospholipids are **amphipathic** substances, that is they are polar molecules with heads which are soluble in water (**hydrophilic**) and long, insoluble (**hydrophobic**) tails. See figure 55.

55   An amphipathic molecule

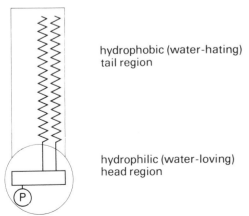

hydrophobic (water-hating) tail region

hydrophilic (water-loving) head region

SAQ 41 If a collection of phospholipid molecules were dropped into a beaker of water, how would they become arranged?

This property of phospholipids was seized on by two Dutch scientists, Gorter and Grendel, in an investigation into the amount of lipids available in red blood cells for their cell membranes.

They extracted the lipids from the membranes of red blood cells with a lipid solvent, acetone. The lipids were then carefully added to the surface of a trough of water where they arranged themselves with their head regions dissolved in the water and tail regions 'sticking up' into the air, as in figure 56.

56   Lipid molecules at an air–water interface

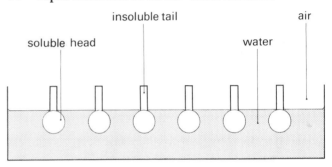

insoluble tail

soluble head

air

water

The water trough was designed so that a moveable piston would be drawn across the surface, pushing together the lipid molecules, as illustrated in figure 57.

57   Gorter and Grendel's apparatus

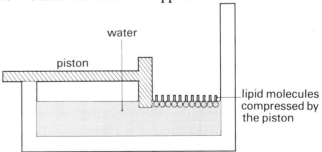

water

piston

lipid molecules compressed by the piston

As soon as the molecules became tightly packed there was an increased resistance to the movement of the piston. The molecules now formed a single layer and the surface area covered by them was measured. They then compared this surface area with the total surface area estimated for the red blood cells used to supply the lipids.

SAQ 42 (*a*) Suggest three reasons why red blood cells were used rather than any other cells in this investigation.

(*b*) What sort of relationship would you expect to find between the surface area of lipids and that of red blood cells if the cell membrane was made up of a layer of lipid molecules?

Gorter and Grendel obtained the following results:

number of cells per cm^3 of human blood = 4.74×10^9

surface area of one cell assuming structure to be
   a disc = 99.4 μm^2

estimated surface area of lipids from 1 cm^3 of blood
   = 0.92 m^2

SAQ 43 (*a*) What is the approximate ratio of lipid to cell surface area?

(*b*) State an hypothesis, consistent with Gorter and Grendel's original hypothesis, to account for this ratio.

Gorter and Grendel concluded that the amount of lipid present was sufficient to cover the total surface of the red blood cells in a layer two molecules thick.

They suggested that the red cell was surrounded by a double layer of lipid with the hydrophilic ends directed to the outside and inside of the cell (see figure 58).

58 A bimolecular lipid layer

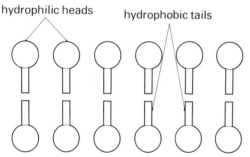

This was the first statement of the idea that a cell membrane is basically composed of a bimolecular lipid layer.

The lipid content alone could not explain all the observed properties of the membrane, and this and other evidence led Danielli and Davson in 1934 to suggest that a layer of protein was adsorbed onto the lipid layer. Over the years they gradually refined

their hypothesis so that the proposed structure of the membrane emerged as shown in figure 59.

59 Danielli and Davson's model of membrane structure

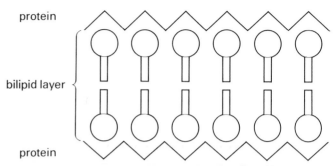

SAQ 44 How could Danielli and Davson's hypothesis be tested?

As well as being consistent with evidence available at the time, a good hypothesis should also lead to certain predictions being made which can be tested.

Danielli and Davson's hypothesis led them to make certain predictions about the width of the membrane. They predicted the following dimensions.

Each protein layer = 1 nm
  Lipid layer   = 6 nm
  Total width   = 8 nm

These predictions were eventually supported from the evidence made available by the measurement and appearance of plasma membrane in electron micrographs.

Electron micrograph 60 shows part of an animal cell magnified 200 000 times. Examine the boundary between the light and dark areas. This is the cell membrane.

SAQ 45 (*a*) Describe the structure labelled above as the cell membrane.

(*b*) Estimate the dimensions of the components of this structure.

(*c*) Relate your estimates to Danielli and Davson's prediction of the dimensions of a cell membrane.

The Danielli–Davson model of the plasma membrane was further developed to incorporate the existence of protein-lined pores, as illustrated in figure 61.

Although these pores were theoretically necessary to explain the passage of certain water-soluble molecules

60 Electron micrograph of an animal cell plasma membrane (× 200 000)

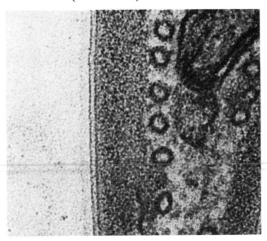

61 Protein-lined pores in the plasma membrane

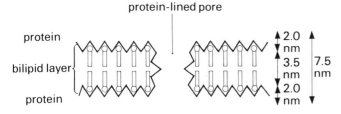

across the membrane, they could not be found in any electron micrographs. Indeed, electron micrographs were revealing that the plasma membrane was not such a uniform structure as predicted by Davson and Danielli and, in particular, it appeared that particles were embedded in the membrane at irregular intervals.

S. J. Singer and G. L. Nicolson also criticised the model because it did not fit the thermodynamic requirements for the best arrangement of molecules present in it. Both phospholipids and proteins are amphipathic and ideally their hydrophilic parts should be in contact with water and their hydrophobic parts away from water.

SAQ 46 In what way did Danielli and Davson's model not comply with the ideal thermodynamic arrangement of membrane molecules?

Singer and Nicolson on reviewing all the available evidence in 1972 constructed what is now the most widely accepted model of the plasma membrane which they have named the **fluid mosaic model**.

This model of the cell membrane consists of a matrix of phospholipid molecules arranged largely in a bilayer, having globular protein molecules dissolved in it at irregular intervals (see figure 62).

62 The fluid mosaic model of membrane structure

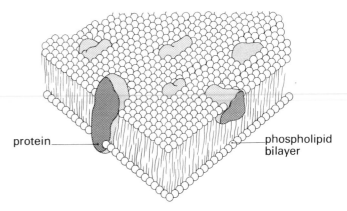

protein ___ phospholipid bilayer

SAQ 47 (*a*) Examine figure 62 and explain how the fluid mosaic model differs from Danielli and Davson's model.
(*b*) Why is the fluid mosaic model a better thermodynamic arrangement of molecules than that of the Danielli–Davson model.

The fluid mosaic model has the hydrophobic amino and fatty acid parts of the proteins and phospholipids positioned away from water molecules whilst the hydrophilic groups are at the membrane surfaces, in contact with water molecules.

The proteins dissolved in the fluid lipid bilayer are called integral proteins and account for at least 70% of the membrane protein. The remaining 30% of proteins are called peripheral proteins and these are normally weakly held to the membrane surface. It appears that the integral proteins may move in the plane of the membrane.

SAQ 48 Explain why Singer and Nicolson called their membrane model the 'fluid mosaic model'.

6.3 Summary assignment 6

Copy figure 63 and annotate your diagram to show the structures and dimensions of the plasma membrane and a summary of the evidence for the fluid mosaic model.

63 A summary of the fluid mosaic model of membrane structure

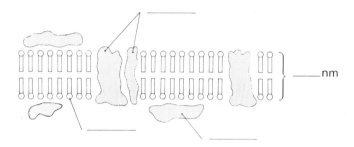

— nm

Show this work to your tutor.

Self test 5, page 85, covers section 6.2 of this unit.

6.4 Movement across a cell membrane

Materials may move across cell membranes in a number of ways. These ways may be classified according to whether or not the cell has to expend energy in causing the movement. If energy is expended, the process is **active transport**, if not, then it is considered to be **passive transport**.

Two methods of passive transport across cell membranes have previously been mentioned. Substances may dissolve in the lipid component of the membrane and dissolve out again on the other side of the membrane; substances which are not lipid soluble may pass through channels in transmembrane proteins. A third passive method also involves protein molecules which combine with certain other molecules and transport them across the membrane without any expenditure of energy.

Active transport, on the other hand, involves the use of energy to move or pump substances into the cell although, once again, membrane proteins are involved in the process.

The process of diffusion is involved in the first two of the above passive methods.

6.4.1 Diffusion

Diffusion is defined as the movement of molecules from a region where they are in high concentration to a region where they are in low concentration No

external source of energy is necessary to cause this movement. This is because all molecules have an internal kinetic energy which means that they are in constant motion. Gaseous and liquid molecules move around randomly within any container holding them and solid molecules are more closely held together and restricted to vibrating backwards and forwards.

Although this molecular movement is random, it can lead to a net directional movement where there is a difference in concentration between two regions. This is illustrated in figure 64 which represents what happens when dye molecules are added to one end of a system containing water molecules.

64 Net movement of dye molecules

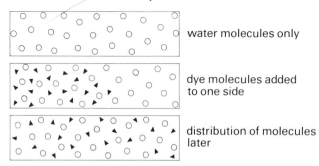

water molecules only

dye molecules added to one side

distribution of molecules later

The dye molecules are moving randomly, but because there are many more in one region than in another, then, purely by chance, more will move from the region of high concentration to the region of low concentration than in the opposite direction. This **net** movement of molecules is described as diffusion. Note that the word 'net' should be used because some molecules also move from low to high, they are simply outnumbered by those moving in the opposite direction.

SAQ 49 (a) When will diffusion stop?
(*b*) When diffusion stops, have the molecules stopped moving? Explain.

The rate of diffusion of any molecule from one region to another is defined as the number of molecules moving between the regions per unit time per unit area.

SAQ 50 How would you expect the following factors to affect the rate of diffusion?
(*a*) the size of molecules
(*b*) the temperature

(*c*) the difference in concentration between two regions

(*d*) the medium in which diffusion occurs

6.4.2 An investigation into diffusion rates

The apparatus illustrated in figure 65 was used in an investigation into the diffusion rates of ammonia from two different concentrations of ammonium hydroxide solution.

65 Apparatus for investigating the rate of diffusion of ammonia

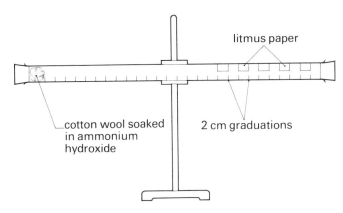

Two sets of apparatus were used which were identical in all respects except that the cotton wool in one set was soaked in 0.2 M ammonium hydroxide solution and in the other set in 0.9 M ammonium hydroxide solution. Ammonia is given off from this solution and diffuses away from it. The time taken for the litmus strip to register the presence of ammonia molecules at each point is shown in figure 66.

66 Table of results for diffusion of ammonia

Distance travelled by ammonia (cm)	Time taken to reach distance (s)	
	0.9 M solution	0.2 M solution
8	37	80
10	65	210
12	120	447
14	163	660
16	280	940
18	385	1325
20	620	1850
22	910	2723
24	1130	3581

SAQ 51 (*a*) Which of the factors which affect rates of diffusion is this investigation concerned with?

(*b*) Plot a graph to compare the rates of diffusion in each tube.

(*c*) Explain how the ammonia travels along this tube. Give the reasons why effects of air currents and convection currents may be eliminated from this explanation.

(*d*) Explain the differences in rate of travel observed between the tubes in terms of particles or molecules.

(*e*) Give reasons for the observed differences in time taken to diffuse the 2 cm between 8 cm and 10 cm, and 18 cm and 20 cm, in the tube with a high concentration of ammonia present.

(*f*) Give brief details of how this investigation could be modified to investigate any of the three other factors previously mentioned which affect the rate of diffusion.

In biological systems we are normally concerned with diffusion across a cell membrane, and for any specific molecule under normal conditions, one of the major variables affecting the rate of diffusion will be the difference in concentration between the outside and inside of the membrane. This difference may be represented graphically as shown in figure 67.

67   Concentration gradients across membranes

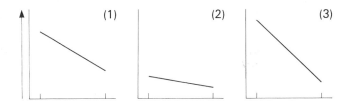

SAQ 52 Which of the graphs in figure 67 indicates the fastest, and which the slowest rate, of diffusion?

The gradient of the graph line indicates the rate of diffusion for the particular concentrations illustrated. The steeper this gradient, the faster the rate of diffusion. When molecules move across a membrane from a high concentration to a lower concentration, they are described as moving down a concentration gradient. Just as boulders run down a hill without needing any force exerted on them, molecules passively move down concentration gradients by diffusion.

SAQ 53 When boulders run down a hill they are converting potential to kinetic energy. What source of energy is involved in molecules moving down a concentration gradient?

6.4.3 Diffusion and energy

Transport by diffusion down concentration gradients across membranes is a passive process as far as the individual cell is concerned, and 'costs nothing' in terms of energy expenditure by the cell.

SAQ 54 (*a*) Which methods of transport across cell membranes involves diffusion down concentration gradients?
(*b*) Describe how certain substances may enter a cell passively without diffusing.

The movement of oxygen across the membranes of the lung and into the blood capillaries is one obvious example of movement of molecules by diffusion.

Of course, diffusion also plays a very important role within cells when molecules move from one region to another.

In living systems it is often important that the net passage of a substance across a membrane should be kept high and mechanisms are present to ensure that the diffusing substance does not accumulate on one side once it has crossed the membrane. For example, in higher animals, the oxygen which has passed into the blood is rapidly carried away by the flow of blood, thus maintaining the diffusion gradient between oxygen in the lungs (high concentration) and oxygen in the capillaries (low concentration).

SAQ 55 What process must be involved where molecules move 'up hill' against a concentration gradient?

6.4.4 Active transport

Active transport can be thought of as an 'uphill movement' against a concentration gradient. By this means, substances from dilute solutions can pass into the cell when the concentration of those substances within the cytoplasm is higher than outside. It requires a direct use of metabolic energy by the cell. If energy-supplying systems are stopped, such as by metabolic poisons, active transport cannot occur.

A considerable number of substances are known to be actively transported by membranes. For example, inorganic ions in the soil pass into root hair cells by active transport. There is a higher concentration of ions inside these cells than in the soil water around them. If oxygen is not available to these cells because of water-logged conditions, this ion uptake cannot take place.

This method can only occur in living cells. An important step forward (in evolutionary terms) was achieved with the development of this kind of process in the primitive cells.

6.5 Summary assignment 7

1 Complete figure 68 to provide a summary of transport methods across a plasma membrane.

68 Summary of transport methods across a plasma membrane

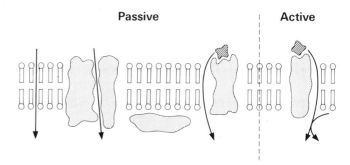

2 Copy out figure 69, which is to contrast diffusion with active transport as a method of moving materials across plasma membranes. Then fill in the spaces under the headings 'diffusion' and 'active transport' with a ✓ or × to indicate which process the items in the list on the left-hand side of the table are involved in.

Show this work to your tutor.

Self test 6, on page 85, covers section 6.4 of this unit.

6.6 Cell membrane simulations

The following practical investigations use Visking membrane, an artificially produced membrane which has similar partial permeability to cell membranes.

	With concentration gradient (diffusion)	Against concentration gradient (active transport)
1 A passive process		
2 Needs the expenditure of energy		
3 Relies on the inherent kinetic energy of molecules		
4 Involves random movement of molecules		
5 Involves a net movement of molecules		
6 Reaches an equilibrium		
7 Is affected by metabolic poisons		
8 Depends on oxygen availablity		

Practical B: The passage of starch

Materials

50 cm³ 1% starch suspension, iodine in KI solution, 15 cm length of Visking tubing softened in water, beaker (250 cm³), distilled water, rubber band, syringe, paper clips

Procedure

(a) Using a paper clip, close one end of the Visking tubing. Use the syringe to add starch solution to the Visking tubing bag, leaving room for the top to be closed firmly by means of another paper clip.

(b) Rinse the outside of the Visking tubing under running water to remove any starch. Place the tube in a beaker containing distilled water. Leave both ends of the tube just out of the water to avoid leakage.

Add enough iodine solution to give the water a distinct yellow colour. (If it turns blue immediately, start again – the membrane is leaking.)

(c) Leave for 10–15 min. Then record any colour change that occurs either in the Visking bag or in the water in the beaker. Present these results in tabular form. (N.B. record original colours also.)

70   **Apparatus for Practical B**

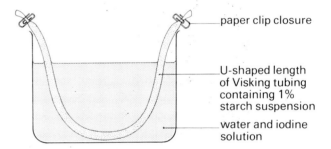

paper clip closure

U-shaped length of Visking tubing containing 1% starch suspension

water and iodine solution

Discussion of results

1 When starch comes in contact with iodine it forms a deep blue colour. On the basis of that reaction, what must have happened to the iodine molecules in the beaker containing water?

2 Which substance (iodine, starch or water) did not pass through the membrane? How did you know it did not?

3 What assumption can you make about the structure of the membrane?

Show this work to your tutor.

Practical C: The passage of water

Materials

Visking tubing, sugar solution (1 mol dm^3), distilled water, 2 syringes, test-tubes, test-tube rack, pins

Procedure

(*a*) Cut your Visking tubing to the same length as your test-tube. Tie a firm knot at one end. Fill with water to check that it does not leak. Empty out the water and use a syringe to half fill it with sugar solution.

(*b*) Push a pin through the top of your Visking tube so that it can be rested across the top of the test-tube. Using the second syringe, carefully add water to the test-tube until the level is exactly the same as that of the sugar solution inside the Visking tube. Tube **A** is now set up.

(*c*) Use a similar procedure to set up tubes **B** and **C** as shown in figure 71.

71 Apparatus for Practical C

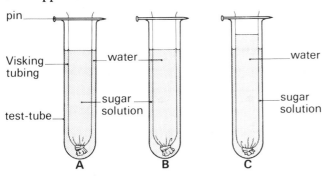

N.B. Water inside the Visking tubing in **C** is a few millimetres above the sugar solution outside it.

(*d*) Leave the tubes for 10 min and then note down the levels in each test-tube. Draw up a table to record initial levels and those after 10 min.

(*e*) If possible, leave the apparatus set up for two hours more and record any change of results.

Discussion of results

1 What is happening in this investigation in terms of diffusion, concentration and selective permeability.

2 Suggest a hypothesis to account for the partial permeability of Visking tubing in relation to molecules of sucrose and molecules of water.

3 If the Visking tube (a partially permeable membrane) is used to investigate an aspect of the behaviour of the cell membrane, which set of apparatus, **A, B** or **C,** is the best model of a cell in water?

4 On the basis of this model, what problems would you expect a protozoan living in fresh water to have? Describe an organelle which might help in overcoming such a problem.

5 Explain any change in results you observed when the apparatus was left for two more hours.

Show this work to your tutor.

6.7 Programmed learning text: The movement of water molecules

In this programmed text, symbols such as ψ^W will be used frequently. When reading such symbols, you will find the text easier to follow if you read them fully as the term they represent. So you would not read ψ^W as 'psi W' but as 'the water potential of pure water'.

The following list of symbols and related terms will prove useful as a reference list if copied out.

ψ^W = water potential of pure water

ψ_s = solute potential

ψ_p = pressure potential

ψ^{SOL} = water potential of a solution

ψ^{CELL} = water potential of cell content

1 All cells are separated from their environment by a plasma membrane. This membrane allows certain molecules to pass through it unhindered whilst preventing the passage of others; it is, therefore, referred to as a selectively, partially, differentially or semipermeable membrane. In this programmed sequence, the term partially permeable membrane (PPM) will be used.

Q What is the function of a PPM?

A A PPM (partially permeable membrane) allows some molecules to pass through it whilst preventing others.

2 An artificially produced material called Visking membrane has partial permeability properties and can, therefore, be used as a model of a cell membrane. The Visking membrane contains pores of limited size which will only allow molecules below a particular size to pass through. This is illustrated in figure 72.

72   Pores in Visking membrane

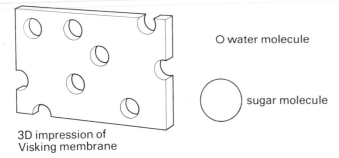

O water molecule

sugar molecule

3D impression of
Visking membrane

(In reality the pores are not all the same size and a few larger pores may be present.)

Q (*a*) Which molecule(s) would pass through Visking membrane as represented in figure 72.
(*b*) What property of membranes restricts the passage of molecules?

A (*a*) Only water is small enough to pass through.
(*b*) The size of the pores in the membrane.

3 Visking membrane may be used to investigate how water molecules move from one solution to another when separated by a PPM. In the investigation shown in figure 73 a tube of Visking membrane con-

73   Investigation of the movement of water

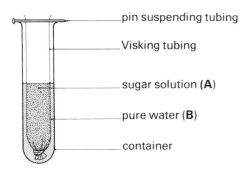

pin suspending tubing

Visking tubing

sugar solution (**A**)

pure water (**B**)

container

taining sugar solution was suspended in a container of pure water. At the start of the experiment the level of the liquid inside the tube was equal to that outside.

Q (*a*) Describe the two liquids under investigation.
(*b*) What separates these two liquids?

A (*a*) **A** is sugar solution consisting of sugar and water molecules. **B** is pure water.
(*b*) The Visking tubing separates the two liquids.

4 After 30 min the levels of liquid in the tubing and container had changed, as illustrated in figure 74.

74   Apparatus after thirty minutes

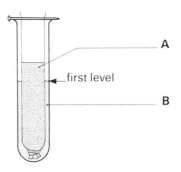

A

first level

B

Q Describe the changes which have occurred.

A The level of the sugar solution **A** has risen, whilst that of the pure water **B** has dropped.

5 The changes in the liquid levels are due to the movement of molecules between them.

Q Which molecules could have moved from the sugar solution to the water, and vice versa?

A Water molecules could have moved in both directions, but the sugar molecules cannot pass through the membrane (or pass very slowly through the few larger pores only).

6 Q If water molecules can move in both directions, how can the change in levels of the liquid be explained?

A More water molecules must have moved from the pure water into the sugar solution than in the opposite direction.

7 Thus, there must have been a **net movement** of water molecules from the pure water to the sugar solution across the partially permeable Visking membrane. Figure 75 explains why this net movement occurs.

All the water molecules are in constant random motion, as are the sugar molecules in figure 75. If, by chance, the water molecules move into a pore, then they will cross from one system to the other. The sugar molecules are, of course, too big to go through these pores. (For the purposes of an investigation such as the one under consideration, movement of the sugar molecules is so very slow it can be ignored.)

75   The movement of water molecules across a membrane

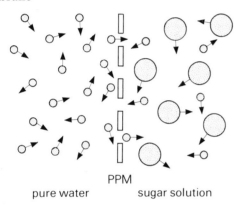

PPM

pure water   sugar solution

Q (*a*) What is meant by a net movement of water molecules?
(*b*) Why do more water molecules pass through the PPM from the pure water than in the opposite direction?

A (*a*) A net movement is the overall movement of water molecules, for instance if six molecules moved from **A** to **B** and three molecules moved from **B** to **A** in a given time, the net movement would be three molecules from **A** to **B**.
(*b*) There are more water molecules per unit volume in pure water than in the sugar solution because part of the volume is occupied by the sugar molecules. By random movement, more water molecules will enter pores from the pure water than from the sugar solution.

8 So, if a partially permeable membrane

separates two solutions having different concentrations of water molecules, there will be a net movement of water molecules from the higher concentration of water to the lower concentration of water. This movement of water is called **osmosis**.

Q Define osmosis.

A Osmosis is the net movement of water molecules from a higher concentration of water molecules to a lower concentration of water molecules across a partially permeable membrane.

9 Consider the diagram in frame 7 again (figure 75). Water molecules are constantly colliding with the PPM. The molecules are, therefore, exerting a pressure on the PPM which means that they are more likely to pass rapidly through a pore when they come into contact with one. Thus, the net movement of water molecules is a result of pressure differences on either side of the PPM. (The sugar molecules will also hit the membrane, though they move more slowly, but this cannot result in movement because the pores are too small for them to pass through.)

Q In which solution, pure water or sugar solution, would you expect the water molecules to be exerting the greatest pressure?

A In the pure water solution, because there are more water molecules, more collisions and, therefore, greater pressure. This is illustrated in figure 76.

76   Opposing water pressures when pure water is separated from a sugar solution by a PPM

pure water   PPM   sugar solution

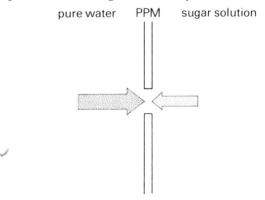

10 In this diagram, the pressure developed by pure water is shown directed through one pore of the PPM. It is resisted by the pressure developed by the water molecules in the solution on the other side of the PPM.

Q Which pressure will be the higher?

A The pressure from the pure water will be higher, leading to a net movement of water molecules from the pure water into the solution.

11 Q Why is the pressure from pure water higher?

A Because of the higher concentration of water molecules in the pure water.

12 *Summary frame*

(1) What is
(*a*) a partially permeable membrane (PPM)?
(*b*) Visking membrane?
(*c*) osmosis?

(2) When a PPM separates pure water from a solution
(*a*) in which direction will water molecules move?
(*b*) in which direction will osmosis occur?
(*c*) in which system will there be a higher pressure exerted on the PPM by water molecules?

A (1) (*a*) A PPM is one which only allows the passage of certain molecules.
(*b*) Visking membrane is an artificially manufactured membrane, having pores of limited size, and thus acts as a PPM in preventing the passage of molecules larger than its pore size whilst allowing the passage of smaller ones.
(*c*) Osmosis is the net movement of water molecules from a higher concentration of water molecules to a lower concentration of water molecules across a PPM.

(2) (*a*) Water molecules will move in both directions.
(*b*) Osmosis, the **net** movement of water molecules, will take place from the pure water into the solution.
(*c*) There will be a higher pressure in the pure water.

13 It is the difference between the pressure exerted by water molecules on either side of the PPM which determines whether or not there will be a net movement of these molecules.

When comparing the pressures of two solutions, the term **water potential**, represented by the Greek letter ψ (psi – pronounced 'sigh') is used.

The water potential of pure water at atmospheric pressure and under isothermal conditions is set arbitrarily at 0. The presence of solutes reduces water potential. Thus, a solution will have a water potential value less than 0, that is ψ^{SOL} will be a **negative** value.

Q You have already seen that the net movement of water molecules occurs from pure water into a solution. Which of these has the higher water potential?

A Pure water ($\psi^{W} = 0$) has the higher water potential. The solution has a negative ψ value and this is thus **less** than 0. Net movement of water is always away from the regions of higher water potential towards regions of lower water potential (the 'downhill' direction.)

14 In the last frame, it was stated that the presence of solutes lowered the water potential of a solution. This is because any addition of solute molecules to either pure water or a solution must reduce the number of water molecules in a unit volume because the additional solute molecules occupy space. With fewer water molecules per unit volume, there will be less pressure exerted by these water molecules. (This is represented in figure 77.)

77 Water pressures of pure water and sugar solution

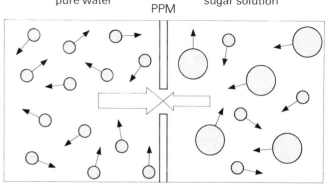

pure water   PPM   sugar solution

The name given to the contribution of solutes to water potential is **solute potential** which is represented by ψ_{s}. At atmospheric pressure $\psi^{SOL} = \psi_{s}$. ψ_{s} is always negative.

Q If one solution contained more solutes than the other, would you expect it to
(a) have a higher or lower water potential,
(b) gain or lose water?

A The solution with more solutes would have a lower water potential and would, therefore, gain water.

15 The water potential (ψ^{SOL}) of a solution is also affected by **pressure** imposed on the solution from outside, as illustrated in figure 78.

78   The effect of external pressure on a solution

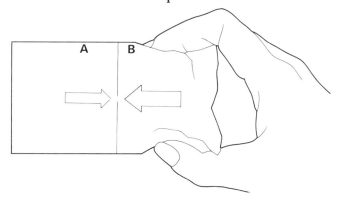

Q If solutions **A** and **B** had equal water potentials ($\psi^A = \psi^B$) and pressure was imposed on **B** (imagine the solution being squeezed), what would be the effect on ψ^B?

A There would be an increase in pressure; ψ^B would be higher than ψ^A and the water would move from **B** to **A**.

16 When pressure is exerted on a system, the water potential is increased by the amount of the imposed pressure.

The name given to any contribution to water potential by external pressure is **pressure potential** and thus is represented by ψ_p.

Q Write an equation to represent the water potential of a solution subjected to an external pressure. Use any or all of the terms ψ^{SOL}, ψ_s, ψ_p in this equation.

A $\psi^{SOL} = \psi_s + \psi_p$
ψ_s is the negative and ψ_p the positive contribution.

17 Q In what units would water potential be measured?

A Units of pressure, newtons per unit area ($N\ m^{-2}$) or, more commonly used in biological examples, bars (bar) or pascals (Pa). For convenience kilopascals (kPa) are generally used.

18 The water potential of a solution is the pressure developed by a unit volume of that solution and is expressed by the formula
$$\psi^{SOL} = \psi_s + \psi_p$$
Figure 79 shows the relationship between the components of water potential of a solution.

ψ_s is a negative pressure. ψ_p is a positive pressure. The combination of these two opposing pressures results in ψ^{SOL}.

79   Relationships between components of water potential of a solution

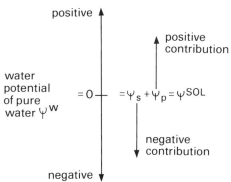

If two solutions were separated from one another by a PPM as indicated in figure 80,

then $\psi^X = \psi_s + \psi_p = -500 + 200 = -300$

and $\psi^Y = \psi_s + \psi_p = -800 + 400 = -400$.

Therefore as $-300 > -400$, $\psi^X > \psi^Y$.

80   Diagram for frame 18

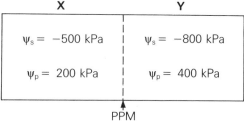

PPM

Q In which direction would there be a net movement of water?

A From solution **X** to solution **Y** (from the higher water potential to the lower).

19 As you can see, use of the term water potential means that you have to work with negative values and this requires some practice.

Q State in each case shown in figure 81, the direction in which there would be a net movement of water.

---

81 Diagram for frame 19

X	Y
$\psi_s = -600$ kPa	$\psi_s = -700$ kPa
$\psi_p = 300$ kPa	$\psi_p = 200$ kPa

X	Y
$\psi_s = -200$ kPa	$\psi_s = -500$ kPa
$\psi_p = 100$ kPa	$\psi_p = 500$ kPa

X	Y
$\psi_s = -400$ kPa	$\psi_s = -400$ kPa
$\psi_p = 200$ kPa	$\psi_p = 300$ kPa

A (a) $\psi^X = -600 + 300 = -300$
$\psi^Y = -700 + 200 = -500$
$-300 > -500$ therefore water moves $\mathbf{X \to Y}$
(b) $\psi^X = -200 + 100 = -100$
$\psi^Y = -500 + 500 = 0$
$0 > -100$ therefore water moves $\mathbf{Y \to X}$
(c) $\psi^X = -400 + 200 = -200$
$\psi^Y = -400 + 300 = -100$
$-100 > -200$ therefore water moves $\mathbf{Y \to X}$

20 *Summary frame*

(1) Define water potential and give its symbol and units of measurement.

(2) How does water potential affect the movement of water between solutions separated by a PPM?

(3) Name two factors which affect water potential.

(4) Write an equation to express the water potential of a solution subjected to external pressure.

(5) State, for the systems represented in figure 82, in which direction you would expect a net movement of water to occur.

82 Diagram for frame 20

X	Y
$\psi_s = -800$ kPa	$\psi_s = -700$ kPa
$\psi_p = 500$ kPa	$\psi_p = 200$ kPa

X	Y
$\psi_s = -400$ kPa	$\psi_s = -300$ kPa
$\psi_p = 600$ kPa	$\psi_p = 500$ kPa

A (1) The water potential of a solution (ψ^{SOL}) is defined as the difference between the pressure exerted by the water molecules of the solution and that exerted by the water molecules of pure water. It is measured in units of pressure, newtons per unit area (N m^{-2}), pascals (Pa) or bars (bar).

(2) Water moves from a region of high water potential to a region of low water potential.

(3) The presence of solutes, the imposition of external pressure.

(4) $\psi^{SOL} = \psi_s + \psi_p$

(5) (a) $\mathbf{X \to Y}$ ($\psi^X = +400 > \psi^Y = -500$)

(b) Neither direction ($\psi^X = +200$, $\psi^Y = +200$)

21 So far, you have considered artificial systems only but, as a biologist, you will be particularly interested in living systems. In this section you will consider the net movement of water with respect to animal and plant cells.

Consider an animal cell surrounded by solution.

Q What kind of membrane surrounds an animal cell?

A Plasma membrane (PPM)

22 Q Under what circumstances will osmosis occur out of or into the cell?

A If $\psi^{CELL} > \psi^{SOL}$, water will move by osmosis out of the cell.
If $\psi^{CELL} < \psi^{SOL}$, water will move into the cell.
If $\psi^{CELL} = \psi^{SOL}$, the solutions will be in equilibrium and there will be no net movement of water.

23 The concentration of solutions surrounding an animal cell is very important. Consider what would happen if an animal cell is placed in pure water.

Q Assuming there is no pressure being exerted on the cell, what would be the expected net direction of water movement?

A There would be a net movement of water into the cell. $\psi^W = 0$. $\psi^{CELL} = \psi_s$ which will be negative (because cytoplasm contains dissolved substances. There are also proteins and other molecules present in the cytoplasm that have an attraction for water and will thus make ψ^{CELL} even more negative.)

24 Q When will equilibrium be reached and osmosis cease?

A Never; as long as some solutes remain in the cell, which they must. ψ^{CELL} will always be negative and less than ψ^W.

25 Q What will be the consequence of this?

A The cell will expand until the plasma membrane ruptures. This is known as lysis and such drastic consequences indicate the importance of reducing water potential differences between an animal cell and its environment.

26 A plant cell differs from an animal cell in having a cell wall and generally a central vacuole, as shown in figure 83.

The cell wall resists internal pressure and thus limits expansion and prevents lysis of the cell. The plasma membrane (sometimes also called the plasmalemma) is the PPM as in animals. The cell wall is usually permeable to water and solutes. For the purposes of water movement in a vacuolated cell, you may consider the plasmalemma, cytoplasm and tonoplast act as a single PPM.

83 A generalised plant cell

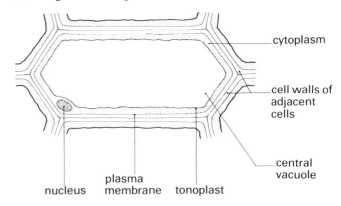

Consider a plant cell immersed in a solution with a greater concentration of solutes present than in the vacuole.

Q What will be the relationship between ψ^{SOL} and ψ^{CELL}?

A $\psi^{CELL} > \psi^{SOL}$

27 Q Describe what will happen to the cell vacuole as a result of this relationship.

A Water will move out of the vacuole by osmosis into the surrounding solution until $\psi^{CELL} = \psi^{SOL}$. The vacuole will shrink because of this loss of water and so will the cell as a whole.

28 The vacuole will lose water to the surrounding solution until ψ^{CELL} is equal to ψ^{SOL}. However, if the two concentrations have not become equal ($\psi^{CELL} \neq \psi^{SOL}$) by the time the cell wall is no longer stretched, the cytoplasm and vacuole will continue to contract and the plasma membrane will lose contact with the cell wall. The cell is then said to be plasmolysed. Such a cell is also described as flaccid, that is the cell wall is not stretched and the whole cell is 'flabby' and soft (see figure 84).

Now consider what happens if a plasmolysed cell is placed in pure water.

Q In which direction will water move by osmosis?

A Water will move into the vacuole as $\psi^W = 0$ and therefore $\psi^W > \psi^{CELL}$.

29 Water will enter the vacuole which expands and pushes the cytoplasm back against the wall. The cell

84 A plasmolysed plant cell

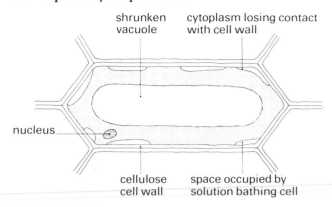

shrunken vacuole
cytoplasm losing contact with cell wall
nucleus
cellulose cell wall
space occupied by solution bathing cell

wall will attempt to resist any further expansion of the cell contents. The pressure exerted by the cell contents on the cell wall is called **turgor pressure**. It starts to force water molecules out of the cell and is therefore equivalent to an external pressure being imposed on the contents of the cell.

Q What will be the effect of turgor pressure on the water potential of the cell?

A Turgor pressure has a positive effect and will, therefore, increase the water potential of the cell. As noted on p48, **16**, the name given to any contribution to water potential by external pressure is **pressure potential**, ψ_p. Turgor pressure contributes to the water potential of a cell and is therefore regarded as a pressure potential (another way of looking at the same problem is to imagine that the cell wall is exerting a pressure on the cell contents which is equal to the turgor pressure).

30 Q Express the relationship between the water potential of the cell and the turgor pressure and solute potential.

A $\psi^{CELL} = \psi_s + \psi_p^{TURGOR\ PRESSURE}$

31 Q When will the ψ^{CELL} be equal to ψ^W?

A When ψ_s is numerically equal and opposite in sign to ψ_p, then $\psi^{CELL} = 0$ and therefore $\psi^{CELL} = \psi^W$.

32 Q What will happen when ψ_p is numerically equal to ψ_s.

A Osmosis will cease (no net movement of water).

33 The plant cell is said to be fully turgid at this

point and pressure potential is at a maximum.

Q If a plant cell was immersed in a solution of water potential − 500 kPa and the solute potential of the cell was − 900 kPa and its wall pressure 300 kPa in which direction would osmosis occur?

A $\psi^{CELL} = \psi_s = -900 + 300 = -600$, $\psi^{SOL} = -500$.
Therefore $\psi^{SOL} > \psi^{CELL}$. Osmosis would occur into the cell from the solution.

34 Q If a plant cell having a pressure potential of 500 kPa and a solute potential of − 500 kPa was placed in a solution of pure water, in which direction would osmosis occur?

A $\psi^{CELL} = \psi_p + \psi_s$
$\psi_p = 500$
and $\psi_s = -500$.
Therefore $\psi^{CELL} = 0 = \psi^W$ (water potential of pure water).
Osmosis would not occur, the cell is fully turgid.

35 *Summary frame*

(1) Under what circumstances will lysis occur in an animal cell?

(2) Write a formula to express the relationship between the water potential of a plant cell, the pressure potential and the osmotic potential.

(3) If a plant cell is immersed in pure water, osmosis will eventually stop.
(*a*) What is the relationship between pressure potential and solute potential at this point?
(*b*) How is the cell described?

(4) Figure 85 represents two adjacent animal cells. In which direction will osmosis occur?

85 Diagram for frame 35

Cell **X**	Cell **Y**
$\psi_p = 900$ kPa	$\psi_p = 600$ kPa
$\psi_s = -1800$ kPa	$\psi_s = -2000$ kPa

A (1) When the cell is immersed in pure water or water having a higher water potential than that of the cell.

(2) $\psi^{\text{CELL}} = \psi_s + \psi_p$

(3) (a) Equal and opposite
(b) Fully turgid

(4) $\psi^X = 900 - 1800 = -900$ $\psi^Y = 600 - 2000 = -1400$

$\psi^X > \psi^Y$ and osmosis will occur from **X** to **Y**.

36 Study figure 86.

86 Water potential in a vacuolated cell

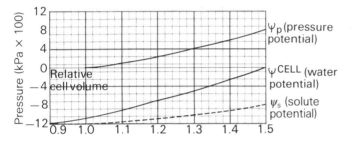

This graph shows the pressure changes that may occur in a vacuolated plant cell.

Q (a) Why is ψ_p always positive?
(b) What term could be applied to the cell when ψ_p = 0 kPa, $\psi^{\text{CELL}} = -1200$ kPa and $\psi_s = -1200$ kPa
(c) What is the cell volume at the point of incipient plasmolysis?
(d) What is the solute potential of the cell at full turgor?
(e) Why do the lines on the graph not extend beyond the points shown on the right-hand side?

A (a) Because it represents pressure potential and this will either be zero (when there is no turgor pressure) or otherwise a positive pressure.

(b) Plasmolysed (flaccid)
(c) 1.0
(d) -800 kPa
(e) Because $\psi^{\text{CELL}} = 0$ and at this point there will be no net entry of water into the cell.

Extension frames

37 So far in this programme, the effects on water

potential of two factors, external pressure and the presence of solute (ψ_p and ψ_s) have been considered. A third factor may be very important when considering the movement of water from soils into plant cells, the uptake of water by seeds and meristematic cells and movement of water into animal cells. This factor is called **matric potential** ψ_m. Macromolecules such as proteins and nucleic acids have an ability to bind water molecules and may generate powerful attracting forces of a chemical or electrostatic nature. The uptake of water by a dry seed (imbibition) is due to matric potential.

Q Will matric potential have a positive or negative value for an animal cell?

A A negative value. The water potential of an animal cell will be lower than could be accounted for by ψ_s alone.

38 Soil particles hold water molecules to their surfaces and this fact contributes to the ψ_m component of the water potential of soil water around a root hair cell.

Q Will this property of soils make it more or less likely that water will enter a root hair cell from the soil?

A Less likely, it lowers the water potential of soil water.

The names given to the pressures involved in water movement in plant cells have differed between groups of biologists and various textbook authors. Figure 87 details the alternative terminology. You

87 Terms used in water relations

Terms used in this unit	Alternative older term
water potential ψ	diffusion pressure deficit, suction pressure
pressure potential ψ_p	turgor pressure, wall pressure
solute potential ψ_s	osmotic pressure, osmotic concentration (these are positive terms, equal but opposite in sign to ψ_s), osmotic potential is another name for ψ_s and is a negative term.

should check with your tutor to see if these terms are required by your examining board or included in any old textbooks you have.

6.8 Control of water content

Whenever a cell is in contact with an aqueous solution, which is virtually always, there is a potential for osmosis. Osmosis will occur if there is any difference in water potential between the cell and the solution. However, the concentration of solutes within a cell is crucial for its efficient operation and, in general, cells have little tolerance for changes in this concentration. They must, therefore, control their water content and osmotic relations with their environment. Control of water content is covered in the unit *Survival – biological themes*.

6.8.1 Effects of osmosis in plant cells

When discussing water relationships of living organisms, the following terms are often used. A **hypotonic** solution is less concentrated than another solution (has a higher, or less negative, solute potential). A **hypertonic** solution is more concentrated than another solution (has a lower, or more negative, solute potential). An **isotonic** solution is of equal concentration to another solution. Although the terms hypotonic, hypertonic and isotonic are sometimes convenient, it is recommended that wherever possible descriptions of solutions should be given in terms of water potential, thus avoiding possible confusion.

Plant cells differ from animal cells in possessing an outer cell wall which resists expansion of the cell contents beyond a certain point. They, therefore, have different osmotic problems from animal cells, as will be demonstrated in the following investigations and text.

Practical D: Turgor in potato tissue

Materials
3 test-tubes, test-tube rack, 2 syringes, cork borer (number 4, 5 or 6), scalpel or razor blade, forceps, potato (10 cm long at least), 0.5 mol dm^{-3} sucrose solution, distilled water, plastic ruler (mm), graph paper covered with plastic film (or callipers), filter paper

Procedure

(*a*) Label three test-tubes. Using syringes, pour 20 cm^3 0.5 mol dm^{-3} sucrose into **C** and 10 cm^3 into **B**.

(*b*) Cut the ends of the potato and use a cork borer to extract three cylinders of potato tissue. Use a pencil to push the cores out. Cut them to the same length of 100 mm.

(*c*) Place one cylinder in each tube. (Make sure that the tube is long enough for the cylinder to be covered by the liquid.) Leave for 24 h. If it is necessary to leave them longer, the tubes and contents should be placed in a refrigerator to prevent decomposition.

(*d*) Remove cylinders with forceps. Dry quickly with filter paper and measure lengths carefully. Note, in each case, whether tissue is firm or flabby. Record all your results.

(*e*) Collate and average the results for your class.

Discussion of results

1 What is the concentration of sucrose in tube **B**?

2 From your knowledge of osmosis in plant cells, what do you suppose has happened to the cells of the potato tissue in water?

3 Explain what might have happened to the cells in the 0.5 mol dm^{-3} sugar solution.

4 Use your answers to these questions to explain the observed changes in length and texture.

5 What will limit the change in length of the potato cylinder immersed in water?

6 What hypothesis could you put forward to account for the result obtained with the potato core in tube **B**?

7 How could this experiment be modified to find out the osmotic concentration of the cell sap?

8 From the texture of your potato cores, attempt to explain (*a*) the value of cell turgor in providing support for plants, (*b*) the cause of wilting in plants.

Show this work to your tutor

Practical E: Water relations of rhubarb epidermis

Materials

Microscopes, slides and cover-slips, dropping pipettes, filter paper or blotting paper, forceps, scalpel or razor blade, small section of rhubarb petiole (red) or onion epidermis, 1 mol dm^{-3} sucrose solution

Procedure

(a) Make a shallow cut in the red outer layer of the rhubarb. With a pair of forceps, lift off a strip of epidermis from the cut. This should be as thin as possible; ideally, you need a layer just one cell thick (see figure 88).

88   Removing an epidermal strip

(b) Place a part of this layer on a microscope slide. Mount in a drop of water and carefully place a cover-slip over it. Examine it under the microscope (× 10 objective). Try to find a group of clearly defined, red-filled cells. If your strip is too thick for any clear cells then start the procedure again.

(c) When you have found a group of clearly visible cells, clip the slide securely to the microscope stage and keep it in position for the remainder of the investigation. Make a drawing of your cells, indicating where red colouration is present.

(d) Place two drops of sucrose solution on one side of the cover-slip so that the liquid just touches the edge. Apply a strip of filter paper to the opposite side of the cover-slip so that the sucrose solution is drawn through.

(e) Observe the cells. If nothing happens, add more sucrose solution and repeat step (d) . When a noticeable change occurs, draw and label the cells as they now appear.

(f) Repeat step (d) using distilled water in place of sucrose solution. Do this twice. Again, record any change with a drawing.

Discussion of results

1 When the sucrose solution was added, what changes did you observe in the shape of the vacuole and the colour of the cell sap within it?

2 What change was there in the overall shape of the cell?

3 Explain the change in the volume and colour of the vacuole.

4 After exposure to the sucrose solution, what occupied the space between the vacuole and the cell wall in the shrunken cells?

5 Why did the cell sap not mix with the liquid in this space?

6 How do the results of this investigation lead to the conclusion that the cell wall is permeable, not only to water but also to dissolved sucrose?

7 What would be the effect on the tissues of the whole plant if all the cells were plasmolysed?

8 What changes took place in the cells when the sucrose solution was replaced by water. Explain the changes in terms of osmosis.

9 If this change occurred in all cells of a plant, what would the effect be on the whole plant?

Show this work to your tutor.

6.8.2 Measuring water potentials in plant cells

One way of measuring the water potentials of plant cells is to place pieces of tissue of known weight into a series of solutions of different solute concentration. A solution which produces no change in weight is considered to have a solute concentration which equals the water potential of the tissue.

SAQ 56 (*a*) From the results in figure 89, what is the molarity of sucrose that brings about no change in weight?

89 Effect of sucrose on a mass of plant tissue

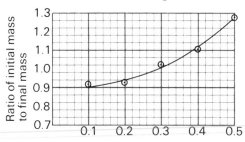

(*b*) What is the water potential of the tissue represented in figure 90?

90 Solute potentials of different molarities of sucrose

Molarity of sucrose (mol dm^{-3})	Solute potential (kPa)
0.05	− 130
0.10	− 260
0.15	− 400
0.20	− 530
0.25	− 670
0.30	− 810
0.35	− 960
0.40	−1110
0.45	−1270
0.50	−1430
0.55	−1600
0.60	−1780

It is more difficult to measure solute potential accurately because it is necessary to eliminate the effects of pressure potential.

A method used involves finding the concentration of an external solution which causes the cells to plasmolyse so that the cytoplasm just loses contact with the cell walls. This state is known as **incipient plasmolysis**. When cells are in this condition there is no pressure from the cellulose wall on the cell contents. Thus, it is assumed that the solute potential of the external solution is equal to the solute potential of the cell sap. In practice, cells tend to plasmolyse at slightly different rates and the practical measure of incipient plasmolysis is taken as the point when half the cells are visibly plasmolysed

(50% plasmolysis). It is assumed that, at this point, half the cells have just plasmolysed and the other half are just about to become plasmolysed.

Small pieces of the inner epidermis of a fleshy scale leaf of an onion bulb were placed in sucrose solutions of different concentrations. After 15 minutes, each piece was examined under a microscope and the percentage of plasmolysed cells in each field determined (see figure 91).

91 Percentage of plasmolysed cells found in different concentrations of sucrose

Molar concentration of sucrose (M)	Percentage of plasmolysed cells
0.55	0
0.60	6
0.65	20
0.70	80
0.75	100

SAQ 57 (*a*) Plot a graph of the results from figure 91.
(*b*) Use the graph to find the molar concentration of sucrose which corresponds to the mean (solute) potential of the cell contents.
(*c*) Give one assumption that is made when using this method of estimating the (solute) potential of these cells.

6.8.3 Osmotic control in animal cells

A number of investigations were carried out in which samples of human blood were added to various concentrations of aqueous solutions of sodium chloride. The resultant mixtures were then examined using a light microscope and some typical results are shown in figure 92.

SAQ 58 (*a*) Describe the control set-up in this investigation.
(*b*) Explain, in terms of movement of water molecules, what has happened in each of the above investigations.

The effects of uncontrolled osmosis on animal cells

92 Shape of red blood cells in three different solutions of sodium chloride

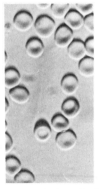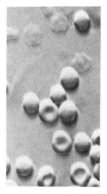

can obviously be devastating. Many types of animal, such as starfish and jellyfish, cannot control the concentrations of their cell and body fluids, which therefore remain equal to the concentration of the surrounding medium. Such organisms are known as **osmoconformers**.

SAQ 59 What disadvantage would this have for these organisms?

In order to avoid this problem, animals have evolved various methods for dealing with excess water intake or output.

SAQ 60 Suggest two possible methods.

The possible mechanisms can be summarised as resistance and regulation.

Resistance involves possession of an impermeable outer layer that will prevent the entry or exit of water.

This effectively eliminates osmosis and a partial use of this method is found in both plants and animals. For example, the possession of overlapping bony scales provides a waterproof outer layer for fish, and many plants have a waxy cuticle on the epidermal layer.

SAQ 61 What problems are caused by having imper- meable outer layers?

Regulation involves possession of some means of gaining a supply of water if too much is lost or of getting rid of excess water from the cell. The former alternative presents the problem of extracting water from the very environment which is causing its

removal from the cell. Some marine species achieve this by 'drinking' the salt water and then excreting the salt.

Regulation has been adopted by many simple organisms which live in an aqueous environment. For example a simple protozoan such as *Amoeba* has relatively concentrated cytoplasm separated from a water medium by its plasma membrane. If the external medium is fresh water, there will be a constant influx of water into the cytoplasm by osmosis. This will dilute the cytoplasm and increase its volume and the animal will swell.

SAQ 62 When would this process reach equilibrium and stop?

Clearly, in organisms of this type, control of the water content (known as **osmoregulation**) of their bodies occurs and the contractile vacuole is the means by which this is achieved. This structure, which accumulates fluid and periodically discharges it, is a well-known feature of most freshwater protozoans but also occurs in some marine forms, in the cells of some unicellular algae and in certain cells of freshwater sponges. The way in which it works is shown in figure 93.

93 Functioning of a contractile vacuole

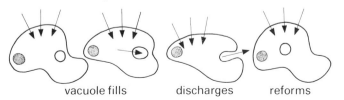

vacuole fills   discharges   reforms

Arrows indicate flow of water

Other aspects of water balance will be considered in the unit *Survival – biological themes*.

Discuss with your group the osmotic problems faced by
(*a*) animals in a seashore rockpool on a warm sunny day;
(*b*) fish in an estuary as the tide rises and falls.

6.9 Examination questions
(AEB, 1979, Paper 3)
In an experiment, the marine ciliate *Cothurnia* was placed in a series of dilutions of sea water and the

output of the contractile vacuole was measured. In another experiment, the change in volume of the organism in different dilutions of sea water was recorded.

The results are given in the table 94.

94 Contractile vacuole output and body volume in relation to salinity in *Cothurnia*

Percentage of added fresh water	Contractile vacuole output (μl s^{-1})	Relative body volume
0	0.65	1.000
10	0.56	1.075
20	1.10	1.175
30	1.00	1.280
40	1.51	1.451
50	2.40	1.600
60	6.31	1.785
70	18.25	2.010
80	35.10	2.092
90	9.55	2.035

(*a*) Plot graphs of these data using a single set of axes.

(*b*) With reference to the contractile vacuole output curve, explain the effects of dilution on the activity of the contractile vacuole.

(*c*) What do the changes in relative body volume indicate about the effect of contractile vacuole activity?

(*d*) Some species of marine protozoa form contractile vacuoles only when the animal begins to feed. Suggest an explanation for this observation.

Show this work to your tutor.

Self test 7, page 85, covers section 6.7 of this unit.

6.10 Extension: Further aspects of cell membranes

Reference: *The Membranes of Animal Cells*. 2nd edition (1978) by A. P. M. Lockwood. Institute of Biology Studies in Biology No. 27.

Read from chapter 4, *A survey of cellular membranes*; section 4.1, page 16, from beginning to 4.1.1 (general form and composition) fourth paragraph (finished at top of page 18); 4.1.2 (cell recognition) page 23; and 4.1.3 (surface interaction) including 4.1.3.1, 4.1.3.2, 4.1.3.3, 4.1.3.4 (pp. 24–29), 4.6, pp. 33–37.

Answer the following questions

1 Describe the form of a kidney cell plasma membrane and the major function of this form (p. 17).

2 What type of molecule is responsible for recognition in cell membranes?

3 In what circumstances may a mutated cell escape recognition by the antibody system?

4 Explain why cancer cells are invasive whilst most cells are not.

5 Name the three main types of intercellular junction.

6 What is the primary function of gap junctions?

7 Make two points of comparison and contrast between gap junctions and tight junctions.

8 Name the primary functions of the lysosome system.

9 Give details of how the lysosome system can lead to disease in men.

Show this work to your tutor.

Section 7 The control of metabolism in cells

7.1 Introduction and objectives

There are thousands of different chemical reactions which occur in living cells. These are known collectively as **metabolism**. The processes of chemical breakdown are called **catabolism**, while the term **anabolism** describes the building up of substances. This hive of chemical activity must be controlled by some mechanism. However, if a particular group of protein molecules, called **enzymes**, did not exist, these reactions would occur so slowly that, effectively, metabolism would cease.

Enzymes act as biological catalysts, which means that they can become involved in chemical reactions and increase the rate of such reactions without themselves being used up.

Enzymes are the immediate agents of control within cells because their activity determines which chemical reaction will proceed quickly enough to have some effect on the cell. However, nucleic acids, in the form of genes, must be considered the ultimate control agents because they determine the type of enzymes present at any particular time.

It is possible to identify up to 500 enzymes within cells although there could be between 10 000–30 000 in mammalian cells. It would be quite inefficient to allow all of these enzymes to drift around the cell catalysing reactions. Although certain enzymes probably do work in this way, there is increasing evidence that many enzymes are organised on plasma membranes or in organelles into efficient groups dealing with related or sequential reactions. The membrane system concerned is called the endoplasmic reticulum, and the principal organelles are the chloroplast and mitochondrion.

A cell may be loosely compared to a factory in the way it regulates its biochemical environment. Like a factory, it has specialised 'machines' which carry out specific tasks. For example, the cell has 'energy generators' (mitochondria) which supply the energy needed for biochemical processes. Also, like a factory, it is divided into production lines (by membranes) and each of these is geared to a particular task. An example of this is the rough endoplasmic reticulum in which proteins are manufactured with the aid of enzymes.

The role of enzymes in the evolution of cells must have been very important for a number of reasons. In this section, you will be considering three aspects of this role. How enzymes increase the rate at which poisonous compounds are broken down, how energy is made available from organic compounds and how compounds needed for cell growth and repair are made.

Whilst considering the role of enzymes as catalysts in the origin of cells, you will also learn how they are involved in their present role of control of metabolism in cells.

At the end of this section you should be able to do the following.

(a) Define the terms enzyme and coenzyme.

(b) Describe the characteristic properties of enzymes in the reactions they catalyse.

(c) Explain a method of enzyme reaction, using the boulder analogy, which involves correct use of the terms:
    energy barrier, activation energy, activation energy threshold and energy level.

(d) Describe the effect of varying conditions of pH, temperature, substrate or enzyme concentration on an enzyme-catalysed reaction.

(e) Describe the lock-key and induced-fit models of enzyme action, using appropriate diagrams.

(f) Explain the principle and operation of a colorimeter, including the use of filters.

(g) Define, and give examples of, cofactors and inhibitors.

Extension

(a) List the modern classification groups for enzymes and the reaction types included in each group.

(b) Describe the techniques used in the study of enzyme-controlled metabolic pathways.

7.2 The breakdown of molecules

The earliest cells had to survive in a very hostile environment. Certainly, they would have constantly come into contact with molecules which would have been extremely damaging had they been able to get into the cell. You have learnt in the previous section how the cell membrane may have acted as a barrier to such substances. However, the cell also has to deal with poisons which do not have to pass the cell membrane barrier to get into the cell.
Certain by-products of a cell's metabolism are poisonous and cells must be able to excrete or break these down very quickly before they damage the cell. Hydrogen peroxide (H_2O_2) is one example of such a poison which is continually formed in cells and broken down rapidly by an enzyme.

Practical F: The breakdown of hydrogen peroxide

In this practical, you will carry out two investigations. Investigation (1) simply demonstrates the effect of liver on hydrogen peroxide.

Investigation (2) involves observing this reaction under different pH conditions ranging from very acidic to very alkaline.

Materials

Test-tubes (8), wood splints, stop-clock, ☠ fresh 3% hydrogen peroxide solution, pieces of raw liver and potato, syringes (1×10 cm^3, 5×5 cm^3), pH paper, forceps, scalpel or razor blade, aqueous solutions of sodium hydroxide (0.1 mol dm^{-3}),

hydrochloric acid (dilute), buffer solutions at pH 4, 7 and 9

Procedure

In all the following tests, assess the rate of reaction as:
0 = no reaction
1 = slow
2 = moderate
3 = rapid

Investigation (1)

(a) Pour 7 cm^3 of 3% hydrogen peroxide solution into three test-tubes labelled **X, Y, Z.**

(b) Add a small amount of liver (the size of a rice grain) to the solution in tube **X**, holding it beneath the solution using a wooden splint.

(c) Add a similarly sized piece of potato with peel attached to the solution in tube **Y**, holding it beneath the solution using another wooden splint.

(d) Tube **Z** is left containing only hydrogen peroxide solution.

(e) Assess the rates of reaction as represented by the rate at which bubbles are produced and record your results in a table.

Investigation (2)

(a) Set up five test-tubes labelled **A, B, C, D,** and **E.**

(b) Add 5 cm^3 of sodium hydroxide solution, pH 9 buffer, pH 7 buffer, pH 4 buffer and hydrochloric acid solution respectively to test-tubes **A, B, C, D** and **E.**

(c) Measure the pH of each solution using pH paper.

(d) Using a different wooden splint and the same-sized piece of liver for each test-tube, break up the liver in the solution in the test-tube.

(e) Leave for 5 min.

(f) Add 2 cm^3 of hydrogen peroxide solution to each test-tube.

(g) Assess the rates of reaction and record your results in a table.

Discussion of results

Investigation (1)

1 What was the apparent rate of reaction of hydrogen peroxide by itself?

2 Describe the effect of adding (*a*) liver, (*b*) potato, on this apparent rate of reaction.

3 What would you predict to be the product(s) of the breakdown of hydrogen peroxide? How could you test your prediction?

Investigation (2)

1 What is the effect of solutions of different pH on the apparent rate of reaction?

2 What was the reason for breaking up the liver?

3 In what ways could the design of this investigation be improved to make the comparison of results more valid?

Show this work to your tutor.

7.3 Extension: Further enzyme investigations

Design investigations which use the method of investigations (1) and (2) (or your improved version of it) to answer the following questions.

1 What is the effect on the reaction of varying the (*a*) temperature, (*b*) hydrogen peroxide concentration, (*c*) mass of liver?

2 Is the enzyme in the liver used up in a reaction?

Your tutor will advise you on whether or when to carry out your designed investigations.

7.4 The boulder analogy

In the previous investigation it has been assumed that an enzyme contained in liver and potato broke down the hydrogen peroxide into water and oxygen, the rate at which oxygen was released being an indication of the rate of the breakdown reaction. Although you would not have noticed any apparent reaction when hydrogen peroxide was by itself, it

does, in fact, slowly decompose to water and oxygen without any enzyme being present. Indeed, it is characteristic of enzymes that they can only alter the rate of a reaction, they cannot make reactions begin.

The reason why hydrogen peroxide will decompose to water and oxygen so very slowly is because there is an energy barrier which impedes its breakdown.

SAQ 63 You have come across the concept of an energy barrier in this unit. Draw a diagram which represents an energy barrier.

Now consider figure 95 which represents the energy changes which occur in the reaction which results in the formation of water and oxygen from hydrogen peroxide.

95   An energy barrier

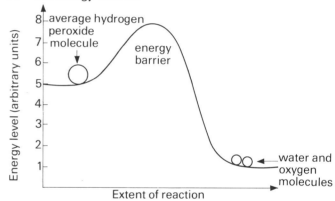

SAQ 64 What name is given to the amount of energy required by the hydrogen peroxide molecule to get over the energy barrier?

Liquid and gas molecules are constantly moving and, as they move, they will collide. In these collisions, energy may be transferred from one molecule to another. So one molecule will gain energy whilst another will lose it. If the energy gain is equal to or more than the activation energy, then the molecule will break down.

SAQ 65 Compare figures 95 and 96. Which, if any, of the molecules shown in figure 96 has sufficient energy to break down?

This collision process may take quite some time; it is dependent on a sufficient supply of higher energy molecules colliding to hoist others over the energy barrier.

two molecules
having different
energy levels

collision

energy transfer
has occurred

One way of increasing the rate of reaction is to heat up the collection of molecules. This raises all their energy levels towards or beyond the activation energy threshold.

SAQ 66 Why is it that biological systems cannot utilise this method to any great extent?

Biological systems use enzymes. Enzymes lower the energy barrier by opening a different pathway for the reaction, which involves the formation of complexes between the molecules involved in the reaction and the enzyme. Returning to the hydrogen peroxide example, look at the energy levels in figure 97 for the breakdown of hydrogen peroxide when an enzyme is involved.

SAQ 67 (a) By how much has the enzyme lowered the energy barrier in the above example?
(b) Consider figure 96. What difference would an enzyme have made to this example?

Graph 97 illustrates that the series of reactions involved when an enzyme is present follows a different pathway which has a lower activation energy threshold. This means that, in any given time, more molecules can attain the threshold and be broken down. Thus, the rate of the reactions can be considerably increased.

To return to the boulder analogy which was originally used in section 5, the effect of an enzyme is to find an alternative route down the hill which goes over smaller humps and thus needs less energy.

Self test 8, page 86, covers sections 7.2–7.4 of this unit.

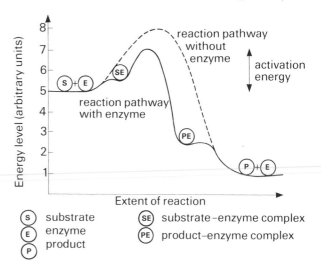

S   substrate
E   enzyme
P   product

SE   substrate–enzyme complex
PE   product–enzyme complex

This section has introduced a number of new concepts. In your small discussion group, make sure that you can explain satisfactorily what you mean by the following terms: biological systems, rate of reaction, the boulder analogy, an energy barrier, activation energy and activation energy threshold.

7.5 Energy release

Cells need energy for many different purposes. They derive their energy from complex molecules which act as energy sources. The reactions which result in the release of this energy are catalysed by enzymes.

In the origin of cells from the primeval soup this particular property of enzymes would have been important, and it is difficult to conceive of any other system by which energy could have been made available in the controlled manner necessary for it to be used by a cell.

Practical G: An enzyme-catalysed reaction

An example of an enzyme-catalysed reaction is the breakdown of starch by saliva. This reaction is the first in a sequence which makes energy available in your own digestive and metabolic system. You will remember that starch suspension, when mixed with iodine/potassium iodide solution, produces a blue colouration. The degree of blueness depends on the concentration of starch in the suspension. So, by adding iodine/potassium iodide solution to samples taken from a mixture of starch suspension and saliva, and measuring the change in blueness of the solution over a period of time, you can follow the course of an enzyme-catalysed reaction accurately.

A device which can be used to measure the blueness of the mixture is the colorimeter which measures the amount of light transmitted through a mixture. Its principle and operation are more fully explained later. The sequence of this investigation will be to

(a) become acquainted with the principle and operation of the colorimeter;

(b) follow the course of a saliva/starch reaction using the colorimeter.

Operation of the colorimeter

The main features of different makes of colorimeter which take liquid samples are similar to those shown in figure 98. Light passes from a bulb via a filter through the sample and onto a photosensitive cell. The deeper the colour of the liquid, the smaller the amount of light falling onto the cell and the lower the reading on the scale.

98 Basic design of a colorimeter

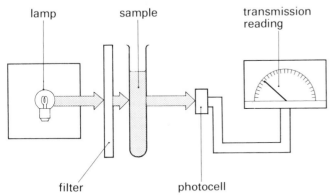

The light filter is important in making the colorimeter more sensitive. A red filter will be used in this investigation because it will only allow red light to pass through it. The sample under investigation will be changing from deep blue to light blue. So, if blue light was used it would simply pass through the sample, but red light will be absorbed and the deeper blue the sample the more red light will be absorbed and the less reach the photosensitive cell.

Colorimeters show either the amount of light transmitted through the mixture or the amount absorbed by the mixture, or both. The scale on your colorimeter which reads from 0 to 100 is the transmission scale, as illustrated in figure 99, which you will use in the following investigations.

99 A colorimeter scale

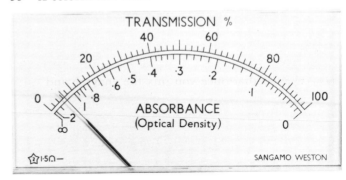

Materials

Colorimeter and red filter, test-tubes for colorimeter, syringes (10, 5, 2, 1 cm^3), beakers (2 × 200 cm^3), stop-clock, water-bath, distilled water, starch suspension (1%) with chloride ions, iodine/potassium iodide solution (0.1% in 2%), saliva solution*

Procedure

*To obtain saliva solution

(a) First rinse out your mouth with water.

(b) Then swill about 25 cm^3 of distilled water around in your mouth for 30 s and collect the solution in a beaker.

(c) Make this volume up to 50 cm^3 with distilled water.

(d) This now forms your stock saliva solution.

N.B. The efficiency of the enzyme in saliva, and amount available will vary between individuals. You may have to adjust the concentration of starch suspension and times at which readings are taken in the following investigations to allow for this. Alternatively, a commercially prepared enzyme may be used.

Following the course of an enzyme-catalysed reaction

This investigation will monitor the amount of starch remaining in suspension as the enzyme catalyses its breakdown over a period of time.

(*a*) Pour 50 cm³ of 1% aqueous starch suspension into a 200 cm³ beaker and stand this in a water-bath at 30 °C.

(*b*) Pour 50 cm³ of saliva suspension into a beaker and stand this in the same water-bath.
You must now prepare the colorimeter and necessary test-tubes so that once you mix the enzyme and starch suspensions you will be able to take samples and record readings efficiently.

(*c*) Place 10 clean test-tubes in a test-tube rack and label them near the top from 1 to 10. The test-tubes should ideally be matched so that they give the same colorimeter readings with the same solution in them.

(*d*) In each test-tube put 1 cm³ of iodine/potassium iodide solution.

(*e*) To test-tube 10, add 10 cm³ of water and use this sample to adjust the colorimeter for 100% transmission with the red filter in position. (Remember to check this reading before and after any other measurements.)

Stages (*f*)–(*i*) must be performed quickly and correctly. Before proceeding further with the investigation, carefully read through the instructions below.

(*f*) Add all the enzyme suspension to the starch suspension and start the stop-clock.

(*g*) At 1 min intervals, remove 10 cm³ of the reacting mixture, using a syringe, and transfer it to the correctly labelled test-tube. (Wash out the syringe with distilled water before re-using.)

(*h*) Mix the contents thoroughly and dry the outside of the tube. Put the test-tube into the colorimeter. Record the reading.

(*i*) Repeat the 1 min sampling until all the reacting enzyme–starch mixture has been used.

It is possible that because of the saliva used, the reaction may have gone too quickly or too slowly to be effectively recorded in ten minutes. You may have to repeat this investigation at different time intervals – check this with your tutor.

(*j*) The readings you record from a colorimeter are measurements of light transmission. In the investigation on the course of an enzyme reaction, you need to know how much starch has been broken down in a given time. So, it is necessary to find out what the light transmission readings of the colorimeter indicate in terms of starch concentration. The procedure for investigating this is called a calibration procedure and will result in a conversion graph similar to graph 100.

100 A calibration curve of starch concentration against light transmission

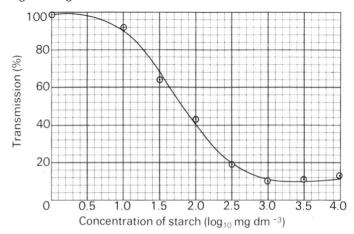

From this graph it will be possible to work out, for a given transmission (*y*), the related starch concentration (*x*) by drawing in the horizontal and perpendicular lines.

Obtain a conversion graph for the colorimeter you have been using from your tutor and convert your colorimeter readings into starch concentrations.

Discussion of results

1 Plot a graph of starch concentration against incubation time (the time during which the reaction has been allowed to take place).

2 Describe the graph you have plotted.

3 At what rate is the starch being broken down in this catalysed reaction?

4 How would you find out the rate at which starch is broken down in an uncatalysed reaction?

5 What information, if any, can be obtained from the graph about the rate of formation of the products of this reaction?

Show this work to your tutor.

7.6 Investigating enzyme kinetics with a computer

The effect of various conditions on the rate of enzyme-controlled reactions is referred to as enzyme kinetics. One of the major problems, which you will now be aware of in investigating enzyme kinetics, is that of time. A lot of time is needed to carry out the series of practicals necessary to give the required data.

The ENZKIN computer simulation program can overcome this time problem to some extent. A group of scientists have worked out how various enzyme-controlled reactions vary with different conditions. They then designed a computer program which would give the end result of such a reaction if certain conditions were specified.

For any of the enzymes investigated, any one of the following conditions may be varied.

(*a*) pH (from 0–14)

(*b*) Substrate volume (from 0–9.5 cm^3)

(*c*) Enzyme volume (from 0–9.5 cm^3)

(*d*) Incubation time (from 0–60 min)

(*e*) Temperature (from 0–100 °C)

In the simulation, you can choose to manipulate one of the above variables and also choose to fix the others at selected values. So, you can design a procedure, inform the computer of the details and it will give you the results in seconds. Your tutor will advise you about the availability of this programme.

7.7 The effect of varying conditions on enzyme activity

By now, you should have carried out practical or computer investigations into the effect of varying certain conditions in which enzyme reactions occur.

The series of graphs below represent the general results from such a series of investigations.

7.7.1 Enzyme concentration

The rate of an enzyme-catalysed reaction is directly proportional to the concentration of enzyme present as shown in graph 101.

101 Enzyme concentration and rate of reaction

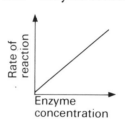

This relationship only holds true if the pH and temperature are kept constant and the substrates (molecules being acted on by the enzyme) are present in excess quantities. The effects of pH and temperature will be explained later.

SAQ 68 Why must the substrate be present in excess quantities?

7.7.2 Incubation time

Incubation time is the time allowed for the reaction to take place. The usual effect of incubation time on the rate of reaction is shown in graph 102.

102 Incubation time and rate of reaction

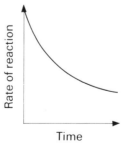

SAQ 69 What consequences does the above information have for the design of investigations into the effect of varying conditions on enzyme activity?

7.7.3 Substrate concentration

If the initial rate of an enzyme reaction is measured

at a series of substrate concentrations, the results shown in graph 103 are obtained.

103 Substrate concentration and rate of reaction

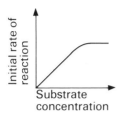

At low substrate concentrations the rate is directly proportional. At high concentrations the rate is constant.

SAQ 70 Why is it important to measure the initial rate above?

7.7.4 pH

Usually, enzymes exhibit catalytic activity only over a narrow range of pH values. Within this narrow range there will often be one particular pH value at which activity is greatest and this is known as the optimum pH value for that particular enzyme. For most enzymes, the optimum pH is between 5 and 9 but there are exceptional enzymes which exhibit greatest activity at extremes of pH. Graph 104 illustrates the typical effects of pH on the activity of two enzymes which are found in the human gut.

104 pH and rate of reaction

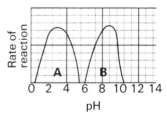

SAQ 71 (a) What is the optimum pH for the two enzymes described?
(b) Would you expect these enzymes to be present in the same part of the human gut? Explain your answer.

7.7.5 Temperature

The rate of an enzyme-catalysed reaction increases directly with temperature, as the rate of any chemical reaction would, but only up to a maximum temperature after which the enzyme activity rapidly diminishes. This loss of activity at 'high' temperatures is irreversible and, as with irreversible loss of activity due to extremes of pH, is called **denaturation**. Graph 105 illustrates this.

105 Temperature and rate of reaction

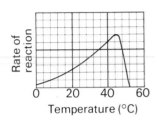

SAQ 72 At which temperature is the highest rate of enzyme activity recorded?

The highest rate achieved is sometimes related to an optimum temperature as with pH. This is not as useful a term in the case of temperature, however, because the denaturation caused by temperature is related to time of exposure. Thus, a longer time at lower temperatures may be more 'inactivating' than a shorter time at higher temperatures. Thus, any concept of optimum temperature must involve consideration of the system and its incubation time, and also its role in metabolism.

SAQ 73 What difference could an enzyme's role in metabolism make to the definition of its optimum temperature?

Self test 9, page 86, covers section 7.7 of this unit.

7.8 A model of enzyme action

You have now investigated the conditions in which two enzymes catalyse the breakdown of their substrates. It has been stated that the enzymes catalyse breakdown reactions because of the way they form complexes with the substrate. However, enzymes are usually very large molecules compared to their substrates and it is therefore not surprising to learn that only a small part of the enzyme makes contact with the substrate. This is known as the **active site** of the enzyme. The following model will show how the active site is involved in catalysis and also the importance of the rest of the enzyme to the active site.

Figure 106 represents an enzyme molecule which has formed a complex with a substrate molecule. The active site of the enzyme is indicated by heavy shading.

106   An active site

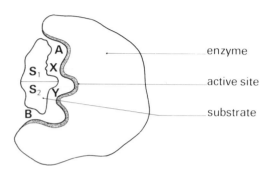

At points **A** and **B** bonds are formed which help hold the substrate molecule in position, whilst at **X** and **Y** bonds are formed which catalyse the breakdown of the substrate into two components S_1 and S_2. When this occurs, the products S_1 and S_2 of the reaction are released from the active site and the enzyme is ready to catalyse another reaction.

When this model of enzyme action was first suggested, it was referred to as the **lock-key model.** This is because a comparison can be made between the way a substrate and enzyme fit together and the way a key and padlock do. Consider figure 107 which illustrates this comparison.

So, in the lock-key model of enzyme action, the enzyme is compared to a key which unlocks the sub-strate releasing its component parts. The model is useful in remembering the basic mechanism suggested for enzyme action and can be extended to account for some of the other characteristics of enzymes.

SAQ 74 Explain how the following characteristics are consistent with the lock-key model of enzyme action.
(*a*) Enzymes are very efficient. They may increase rates of reactions by factors of 10^9 to 10^{12}. Extremes of physical conditions would be required in order to produce such increases without enzymes. For

example, the fixation of nitrogen in bacteria happens at soil temperature and pressure but the Haber process requires $400\,°C$ and 800 atm to carry out the same process using the best available inorganic catalysts.

107   The lock–key model of enzyme action

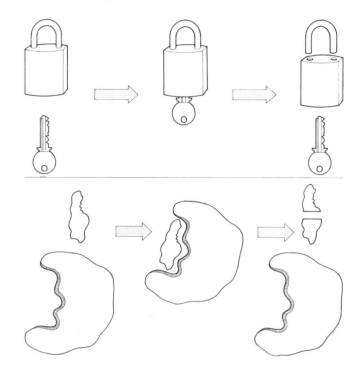

(*b*) Enzymes are specific. They will only act on one or a few chemically related compounds. For example, lactic acid can exist in two forms, called isomers, which have slightly different structural formulae. One enzyme found in bacteria will catalyse the oxidation of one form of lactic acid but not the other.
(*c*) Enzyme shape is important to function. If the shape of an enzyme, which is determined by its tertiary structure, is affected by high temperatures or extremes of pH, for example, it loses its activity. The process is called denaturation.
(*d*) Enzyme reactions are reversible: if an enzyme can catalyse a reaction in one direction, such as
$S \rightarrow S_1 + S_2$, then it will also be able to catalyse the reverse reaction, that is $S_1 + S_2 \rightarrow S$.
(*e*) Enzymes are not used up or destroyed by the reactions they catalyse.

7.9 Enzymes and synthesis

So far, you have dealt with enzymes involved in breaking down molecules. However, enzymes also carry out the reverse reactions, building-up or synthesis of molecules.

Living cells require large numbers of protein molecules for their structure and function. The production of these molecules from amino acids is greatly speeded up by the action of enzymes.

The amino acids must first be activated by specific activator enzymes. ATP and transfer RNA molecules are also required.

Equation 1

amino acid + ATP + tRNA $\xrightarrow[\text{activator enzymes}]{\text{specific}}$ amino acid-tRNA complex + AMP + pyrophosphate

(AMP is adenosine monophosphate)

The reaction illustrated in equation 1 will occur only if the reactants have sufficient energy to reach the activation energy threshold and if they meet at the correct angle and concentration for the necessary bonds to form.

The activator enzyme can increase the rate of reaction by forming a complex with the reactant molecules at the active site as shown in figure 108. Two amino acids may be joined together to form a dipeptide. This reaction is catalysed by the enzyme peptidyl transferase. Subsequent addition of amino acids, again catalysed by the enzyme, will result in the formation of a polypeptide chain.

Equation 2

amino acid + amino acid $\xrightarrow[\text{transferase}]{\text{peptidyl}}$ dipeptide

In the reaction illustrated in equation 2, the enzyme peptidyl transferase will form a complex with two amino acids to catalyse their combination and produce a dipeptide in a similar way to that shown for equation 1 in figure 108.

108   An enzyme–substrate complex

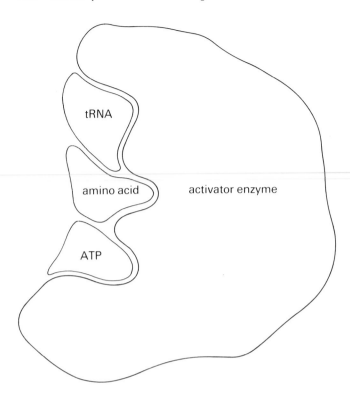

SAQ 75 In what ways could the activity of the enzyme illustrated in figure 108, increase the rate of reaction?

A refined version of the lock-key model called the **induced-fit model** also suggests another way in which the enzyme could catalyse the reaction.

In this model, the enzyme is regarded as having a flexible framework, which can alter in shape. When substrate molecules come into contact with the active site of the enzyme, its shape changes. As a result, the active site is transformed to its most effective catalytic shape.

SAQ 76 Why would this model be more effective than the lock-key model?

7.10 The classification and nomenclature of enzymes

A number of enzymes have been referred to in this section but none of these have been named. The nomenclature (naming) and classification of enzymes is a little confused at present. Some enzymes have three different names by which they are known. Indeed, the enzyme found in saliva is such a case; it is known variously as ptyalin, salivary amylase and α-1,4-glucan-4-glucanohydrolase.

The last of these names is the systematic name which was established by an international commission on enzymes, and it is a useful name in that it describes what the enzymes does. This particular enzyme hydrolyses the α-1,4-glucan link in polysaccharides. The other names mentioned, ptyalin and salivary amylase, are called trivial names and are still extensively used.

The international commission divided enzymes into six general groups:
1 oxidoreductases
2 transferases
3 hydrolases
4 lyases
5 isomerases
6 ligases
and each enzyme is named so that the nature of the reaction involved is described as accurately as possible.

The enzyme involved in the reduction of hydrogen peroxide is therefore called hydrogen peroxide: hydrogen peroxide oxidoreductase. In this reaction, two molecules of hydrogen peroxide combine in a reduction reaction to oxygen and water:

$$H_2O_2 + H_2O_2 = O_2 + 2H_2O$$

Your tutor will advise you about the kind of knowledge you need about enzyme classification and nomenclature. However, in this and successive ABAL units, both the systematic and trivial names will be given.

7.11 Cofactors and inhibitors

A number of relatively small molecules which are not proteins have significant effects on the rate of enzyme-catalysed reactions. Some of these are necessary for enzyme activity and are called **cofactors**, whilst others prevent or diminish enzyme activity and are called **inhibitors**.

Cofactors may be either coenzymes or activators. **Coenzymes** have a specific role in the reaction mechanism and appear in the equation representing the reaction, as shown in the two examples below. Coenzymes are regenerated to their original form after the reaction.

1   $CH_3CH_2OH + NAD^+ \rightleftharpoons CH_3CHO + NADH + H^+$

2   $ATP + glucose \rightleftharpoons ADP + glucose\text{-}6\text{-}phosphate$

The coenzyme involved in reaction (1) is nicotinamide adenine dinucleotide (NAD). NAD acts as an hydrogen acceptor in many of the cell's oxidation reactions (the oxidation of alcohol to acetaldehyde, shown above, is a typical example). The nicotinamide part of NAD is derived from nicotinic acid which is a vitamin.

Indeed, vitamins are known to form various coenzymes and the effects of deficiency diseases caused by lack of certain vitamins is often due to the disruption of metabolic pathways caused by the absence of coenzymes.

Adenosine triphosphate (ATP) is the coenzyme involved in reaction (2) above where it is acting as a phosphate group donor in the phosphorylation of glucose.

Activators, in contrast to coenzymes, do not appear as individual participants in a reaction but are essential components of the active site of the enzyme. They are often metal ions such as zinc, iron or copper.

For example, iron (Fe^{++}) is the activator responsible for the action of hydrogen peroxide: hydrogen peroxide oxidoreductase (catalase) in the reaction:

$$H_2O_2 + H_2O_2 \rightleftharpoons O_2 + 2H_2O$$

Inhibitors act by forming complexes with the enzyme. There are two general types, **irreversible** and **reversible**. Irreversible inhibitors form covalent bonds which are difficult to break and therefore permanently inactivate the enzyme. Arsenic, mercury and silver are poisonous because they irreversibly inhibit important metabolic reactions.

Reversible inhibitors may be divided into three categories: competitive, non-competitive and allosteric. Competitive inhibitors resemble the substrate molecule and compete in binding to the active site of the enzyme. Non-competitive inhibitors interfere with the catalytic part of the active site and, though allowing binding with the substrate, prevent catalysis. Allosteric inhibitors combine with a secondary site on the enzyme away from the catalytic site and produce changes in shape which affect the activity of the enzyme.

A typical example of competitive inhibition is the effect of malonate on the enzyme succinate oxido-reductase (succinate dehydrogenase) which catalyses the oxidation of succinate to fumarate:

$$
\begin{array}{ccc}
\text{COOH} & & \text{H} \quad \text{COOH} \\
| & & \diagdown \; \diagup \\
\text{H--C--H} & & \text{C} \\
| & + \text{FAD--Enz} \rightleftharpoons & \| \qquad + \text{FADH}_2\text{--Enz} \\
\text{H--C--H} & & \text{C} \\
| & & \diagup \; \diagdown \\
\text{COOH} & & \text{HOOC} \quad \text{H}
\end{array}
$$

succinic acid   fumaric acid

$$
\begin{array}{l}
\text{COOH} \\
| \\
\text{H -- C -- H} \qquad \text{malonic acid} \\
| \\
\text{COOH}
\end{array}
$$

Malonate has a similar structure to succinate and therefore competes in binding with the enzyme.

The impression may be formed that inhibitors are always harmful to a cell's metabolism because they interfere with it. This is not the case because they can be very useful as agents of control. A good example of this is the control system in which the products of a reaction act as inhibitors of that reaction. This ensures that the reaction is switched on and off according to the level of product in the cell and thus ensures a relatively constant level of supply of the product according to need.

See if you can explain the following terms to the other members of your discussion group: lock-and-key and induced-fit theories of enzyme action, enzyme inhibition, denaturation, coenzymes, effects of enzymes on rates of reaction.

7.12 Summary assignment 8

Summarise your knowledge of cofactors and inhibitors with an annotated diagram of an enzyme and related cofactors and inhibitors. The scheme shown in figure 109 could be used as a skeleton for your summary.

109   A summary of cofactors and inhibitors

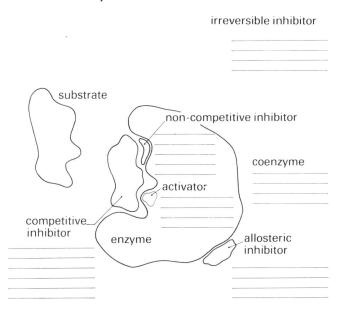

Show this work to your tutor.

Self test 10, page 86, covers sections 7.5–7.8 of this unit.

7.13 Extension: The structure and function of enzymes

Read the following extracts from *The Structure and Function of Enzymes* by Colin H. Wynn. Institute of Biology Studies in Biology No. 42.

Chapter 1, section 1.1, p. 1.
Chapter 3, section 3.2, pp. 23–26.
Chapter 4, sections 4.2, 4.3, 4.4, 4.6, 4.7, 4.8, pp. 41–49.
Chapter 5, sections 5.4, 5.5, 5.6, pp. 56–59.

Then answer the following examination questions.

(*a*) What is meant by (i) an enzyme, and (ii) a metabolic pathway?

(*b*) Give some account of the factors that affect the rate of enzyme-catalysed reactions.

(*c*) Describe two of the techniques that are used in the study of metabolic pathways.
(University of London, 1980)

How would you measure the rate of a reaction catalysed by a named enzyme? Explain what is meant by (*a*) denaturation of an enzyme, (*b*) enzyme inhibition.

One of the most distinctive features of enzyme activity is its specificity. Explain this specificity by reference to the structure and mode of action of an enzyme.

(Oxford and Cambridge Schools Examination Board 1980)

Show this work to your tutor.

7.14 Past examination (essay) questions

Answer one of the following questions.

1 (*a*) What is an enzyme?
(*b*) List the factors which affect the rate of an enzyme-controlled reaction.

(*c*) Describe an experiment to investigate the effect of **one** factor on the rate of an enzyme-controlled reaction.
(*d*) What is meant by a coenzyme? Discuss briefly the role of coenzymes in metabolism.

2 (*a*) What do you understand by the terms (i) enzyme, and (ii) coenzyme?
(*b*) Explain how the following properties of enzymes are a consequence of the structure of enzyme molecules and their mode of action:
(i) substrate specificity, (ii) inhibition, (iii) temperature inactivation.
(*c*) Briefly explain the form in which information for enzyme formation is stored in the cell.

(Joint Matriculation Board, 1979)

3 Select two of the following factors: activators, pH, temperature. For each factor that you choose:
(*a*) describe an experiment which illustrates the relationship between the factor and the rate of enzyme action,
(*b*) indicate how the effects that you describe are brought about.

(University of Cambridge Local Examinations Syndicate, 1979)

Show this work to your tutor.
(London, 1977)

Section 8 Cell growth, reproduction and co-operation

8.1 Introduction and objectives

In the previous three sections you have seen how the pre-cell may have evolved systems and mechanisms which enabled it to control and organise its internal activities and its inter-relationships with its environment. The ultimate control of these systems and mechanisms rests in the molecules of nucleic acid which constitute the cell's genes. These nucleic acid molecules also provide the final missing link which separates the pre-cell from the cell as defined by cell theory. They are capable of precise duplication and subsequent segregation into two separate cells; they therefore allow cells to reproduce themselves.

In this section you will see that unicellular organisms are limited by various factors in their growth and development. Reproduction ensured that unicellular organisms could survive in time and it also allowed for the evolution of multicellular organisms in which cells could cooperate to overcome the limitations of unicellular organisms in growth and development.

After working through this section you should be able to do the following.

(*a*) Define the terms individual and population growth.

(*b*) Account for limitations to cell size in terms of the surface area to volume ratio and flow rates.

(*c*) Explain briefly how the ratio of nuclear surface area to volume of cytoplasm may also limit cell size.

(*d*) List and describe the three major stages of the mitotic cell cycle and the four phases of mitotic nuclear division.

(*e*) State examples of the time taken for the cell cycle and each component stage in at least two different organisms.

(*f*) Describe, in words and diagrams, the mechanism by which mitotic nuclear division occurs and, in par-

ticular, the structure and function of the spindle and the appearance of the chromosomes at different stages in the cell cycle.

(*g*) Describe the differences between plant and animal cells during cytokinesis.

(*h*) Recognise the phase of mitosis from sketches or photomicrographs.

(*i*) Explain what is meant by, and give examples of, plant and animal tissues.

Extension

(*a*) Describe the processes involved in the evolution of the earliest cells.

8.2 Growth

Growth may be defined in two quite distinct ways, both of which are quantitative. **Individual growth** is a permanent increase in the biomass of a cell or organism. **Population growth** is an increase in the number of individuals in a population. If a process is described simply as growth, then this will indicate that individual growth is referred to.

All unicellular organisms are small. The largest are just visible to the naked eye but the great majority can only be seen under a microscope. The factor which appears to limit cell size is the surface area to volume ratio of the cell and nuclear membranes.

A living cell is constantly taking in dissolved substances from its environment and returning them to it as the waste products of its own metabolism. The extent to which substances can pass in and out of the cell will depend on the surface area of the cell membrane, but the extent of the needs of the cell depends on the volume of the cell. If cell metabolism uses certain substances more quickly than fresh supplies can enter, the activities within the cell must slow down or stop. So, the relationship between the area of the cell surface and volume of cell contents can be critical.

This relationship can be illustrated for a growing cell by considering a hypothetical cell which is cuboid and increases its linear dimensions from 1 unit to 2 units and then to 3 units, as shown in figure 110.

110   Increasing size of cells

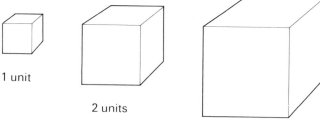

1 unit

2 units

3 units

SAQ 77 Construct a table which shows the consequent increases in surface area and volume as the cell grows and the ratio between the surface area and volume at each stage.

So, as linear dimensions increase, the surface area to volume ratio decreases.

SAQ 78 Do small cells have a greater or smaller surface area to volume ratio than large cells of the same shape?

Consequently, when the linear dimensions of a cell are doubled its need for raw materials rises by a factor of eight, but the surface area through which they must pass is only quadrupled. Either the flow rate must be doubled or the cell's activities must diminish, and as there are limits to both of these options there is a limit to the size of unicellular organisms.

SAQ 79 How might the ratio of nuclear membrane surface area to cell volume put a limitation on cell size?

So, there would appear to be an upper limit to the amount of cytoplasm which can be effectively controlled by a single nucleus. Some organisms have many nuclei within bodies that are not divided into single cells. These show vigorous streaming movements of the cytoplasm which may circulate chemical substances and produce coordination of the activity of the nuclei. This is one possible solution of the size

problem, but it is not widely adopted, and even so these organisms do not grow beyond a few millimetres.

The effect of increasing size on the entry of substances due to diffusion can be demonstrated by a simple investigation.

Practical H: Diffusion and size

Materials

Small crystallising dish containing 2 cm depth of agar jelly, potassium permanganate solution, 2 beakers (100 cm³), scalpel or razor blade, blotting paper or filter paper

Procedure

(*a*) Cut out cubes of jelly of the following lengths of side: 20 mm, 10 mm, 5 mm. Place these cubes in a small beaker and cover with the potassium permanganate solution. Leave for 5 min.

(*b*) Pour off the potassium permanganate solution into another beaker. Dry the surfaces of the cubes thoroughly with blotting paper. Then cut each cube in half and examine the cut surfaces.

(*c*) Record your observations in tabular form. Explain your observations as fully as you can.

Show this work to your tutor.

Growth is a characteristic of living cells, but it should now be clear that cells cannot continue to grow indefinitely since the surface area to volume ratio must impose a limit. One solution to this problem is the division of the growing cell into two cells. If both of these grow, they can attain together a larger volume than the single cell, since they will have twice the surface area.

8.3 Mitosis

The process by which unicellular organisms, and the individual cells of multicellular organs, divide into two cells is called **cell division** and the associated nuclear division which occurs is called **mitosis**.

AV 5: Mitosis in the endosperm of *Haemanthus katherinae*

Materials

VCR and monitor
ABAL video sequence: *Mitosis*

Procedure

View the film two or three times and observe the activity of the cells undergoing mitosis. Mitosis is a continuous process which is arbitrarily divided into phases so that it can be described easily. Although you will be studying mitosis with reference to these phases, you should not forget the reality revealed in the film.

Next, you will study the details of mitosis in a programmed text, after which you will be able to observe the film more carefully and describe the events accurately.

8.4 Programmed learning text: Somatic cell division

1 Multicellular animals and plants grow by increasing the number of cells which make up the individual organism. The process responsible for this growth is **mitotic cell division** in which a single parent cell divides to form two identical daughter cells. These daughter cells may, after a period of preparatory activity called **interphase**, become parent cells themselves and undergo cell division.

Q Fill in the missing words below.

The process of _____ cell division is responsible for _____ in multicellular organisms. It involves a single _____ cell dividing into two _____ daughter cells and is preceded by a preparatory phase called _____.

A Mitotic, growth, parent, identical, interphase.

2 Cell division can be considered as a division of nuclear material called mitosis, followed by a division

of cytoplasmic material called **cytokinesis**.

Q In the correct sequence, list the three stages a somatic cell would undergo in producing two daughter cells.

A Interphase → Mitosis → Cytokinesis

3 The time taken for a complete cycle of events (the cell cycle) varies from organism to organism, and cell type to cell type, and is dependent on environmental factors such as temperature. A few typical times are indicated in table 111.

111   Cell cycle times for different cells and conditions

Cell type	Temperature (°C)	Cell cycle time (h)
Human muscle cell	20	18.00
Grasshopper nerve cell	38	3.50
	26	8.00
Tradescantia stamen cell	10	2.25
	45	0.50
Bacterium	37	0.25
Root tip cells	20	22.00

Q (*a*) Which are the fastest and slowest examples given in table 111?
(*b*) What appears to be the effect of temperature on the cell cycle?

A (*a*) Fastest – bacteria taking 15 min, slowest – root tip cells taking 22 h.
(*b*) The cell cycle is quicker at higher temperatures.

4 Generally speaking, interphase takes a relatively long time in comparison to the other stages of the cell cycle. A typical example of the relative times taken by the stages is illustrated in figure 112.

Q How much longer is interphase than mitosis?
(*a*) × 2 (*b*) × 5 (*c*) × 10 (*d*) × 20

A × 10

5 A mitotic cell cycle leads to a rapid increase in the number of cells in an organism. An example will illustrate this.

112 The cell cycle

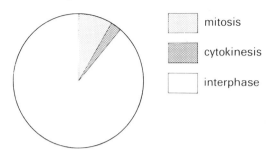

mitosis

cytokinesis

interphase

Q If interphase took 11 h and cell division 1 h, what is the maximum number of cells which could be formed from one parent cell in 7 days? Is it (*a*) less than 1000, (*b*) between 1000 and 10 000, (*c*) between 10 000 and 100 000, (*d*) greater than 100 000?

A (*c*) between 10 000 and 100 000

6 Figure 113 illustrates how such a large number can be formed so quickly from one original cell.

113 Doubling of cell number in mitosis

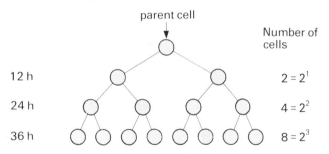

parent cell

Number of cells

12 h $2 = 2^1$

24 h $4 = 2^2$

36 h $8 = 2^3$

Q How many cells will there be in the population after 7 days? (Express your answer as 2^x.)

A 2^{14} (or 16,384)

7 All these cells will be similar to the original parent cell and their chromosomes will be identical copies of those in the parent cell.

Q If the chromosomes in a parent cell are to be identical in structure and number to those in a daughter cell, what must happen in the parent cell before cell division?

A The chromosomes of the parent cell must be duplicated so that there are two identical sets, one for each daughter cell.

8 The duplication of chromosomes which are to be passed on to the daughter cells occurs during interphase. This is a period of intense activity in preparation for division. The interphase cell, under the microscope, has a very similar appearance to any non-dividing cell. This is because the chromosomes are not visible during interphase (they are believed to be in the form of long thin threads).

Q (*a*) How does the interphase cell differ from the non-dividing cell?
(*b*) Would you expect a high or low metabolic rate during interphase?

A (*a*) The interphase cell is different because the chromosomes are being duplicated, even if this is not visible.
(*b*) A high metabolic rate is typical of interphase cells preparing for cell division. This is due to the considerable amount of synthetic activity going on.

9 Interphase is followed by mitosis which, for convenience, can be divided into four sequential stages: prophase, metaphase, anaphase and telophase. This naming of stages in mitosis can give a false impression of a series of separate acts; however, the whole process is continuous.

Q What phase would follow telophase in a dividing cell?

A Cytokinesis (and then interphase).

10 *Summary frame*

Q Fill in the missing words below.

The _____ cells of multicellular animals undergo a life-cycle in which parent cells divide to form two _____ daughter cells. The life-cycle is described as a _____ life-cycle because of the type of nuclear division which occurs during it, called _____. Although the whole cycle is a series of _____ events, it may be conveniently described in terms of three major stages: _____ in which the cell prepares for division, mitosis in which the _____ divides and _____ in which the cytoplasm divides.

A Somatic, identical, mitotic, mitosis, continuous, interphase, nucleus, cytokinesis.

11 The most obvious event which occurs during prophase, and signals the beginning of mitosis, is the condensing of the long, thin chromosomes into shorter, fatter chromosomes.

Q How would you expect a prophase cell to differ microscopically from an interphase cell?

A The chromosomes, having condensed, would be visible in a prophase cell.

12 Now that they are visible, each chromosome can be seen to consist of pairs of threads lying close to each other. Each member of a pair is called a **chromatid** and they appear to be joined or closely associated in a region called the **centromere** (see figure 114).

114   A chromosome consisting of a pair of chromatids

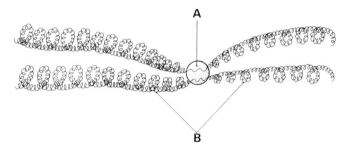

Q (*a*) Which parts of the chromosome are labelled **A** and **B**?
(*b*) For a cell which normally had four chromosomes, how many chromatids and centromeres would you expect to see at prophase?

A (*a*) **A** – centromere, **B** – a chromatid
(*b*) You would expect 8 chromatids and 4 centromeres (see figure 115).

115   A cell in prophase

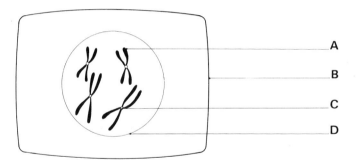

13 Q What structures are labelled **A, B, C** and **D** in figure 115?

A   A – chromatid, **B** – cell membrane, **C** – centromere, **D** – nuclear envelope

14 Another important event which occurs in prophase is the organisation of a structure called the **spindle** (see figure 116). The two ends of this structure are called the poles and the middle region the equator. Between the poles and the equator, very thin, thread-like structures, spindle fibres, are visible.

116   A cell in late prophase

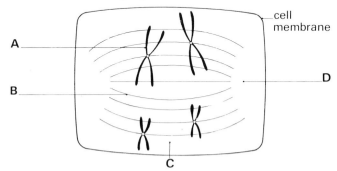

Q What structures or regions are labelled **A, B, C** and **D** in figure 116?

A   A – chromatid, **B** – spindle fibres, **C** – equator, **D** – pole

15 Compare figure 116 in frame 14 with figure 115 in frame 13.

Q What structure is missing from figure 116 which was present in figure 115?

A The nuclear envelope is missing because this breaks down and disappears towards the end of prophase.

16 Structures which are not shown in either figures 115 or 116 are the centrioles. **Centrioles** are a pair of short rods found in the cells of all animals and certain plants. They appear to be associated with the formation of the spindle.

During interphase, two pairs of centrioles are formed from a parent pair outside the nucleus. During prophase, one pair migrates to each pole of the spindle and spindle fibres appear to originate or terminate here (see figure 117).

117 Two centriole pairs with spindle fibres

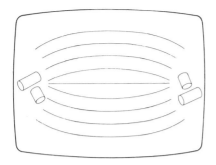

Q Copy out figure 117 and draw in the chromosome pairs correctly. Label your drawing.

A Your labelled drawing should look like figure 118.

118 Late prophase

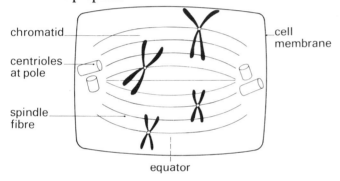

chromatid

centrioles at pole

spindle fibre

cell membrane

equator

17 *Summary frame*

Q Fill in the missing words.

Prophase is the _____ phase of _____ division in which the chromosomes, consisting of paired _____ duplicated during interphase, are condensed into short, fat shapes, thus becoming visible under a microscope. These identical chromatids are joined together at the _____ where they are also attached to a _____ _____. The spindle fibres are associated at the poles of the spindle with paired _____ and spread across the cell, the middle region being referred to as the spindle _____.

A First, mitotic, chromatids, centromere, spindle fibre, centrioles, equator.

18 Immediately after the breakdown of the nuclear envelope, the paired chromatids migrate to the equator of the spindle where they are each attached to a different spindle fibre by their centromeres. This

phase is referred to as a metaphase.

Q Copy out figure 118 but draw in the four paired chromatids as they might appear at metaphase.

A Your drawing should look like figure 119 (although it may not be identical). Points to check are:
(i) have you drawn **paired** chromatids?
(ii) are the centromeres **only** attached at the equator to a fibre?
(iii) are they each attached to different fibres?

119 Metaphase

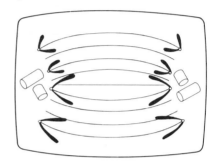

19 During the next stage of mitosis, anaphase, the centromere appears to divide or split into two centromeres and the chromatids are pulled apart by contraction of the spindle fibres in this region.

Q Copy figure 119 but draw the chromosomes in as they would appear during anaphase.

A Your drawing should look like figure 120.
Note that the chromatids are separated and the total number of centromeres is doubled by their splitting.

120 Anaphase

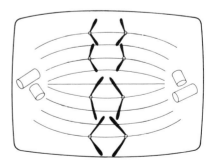

20 Once the paired chromatids have separated, each is referred to as a chromosome. In figure 120 you can see that those chromosomes which were previously paired as chromatids, move to opposite poles.

This is very important because it ensures that there are two sets of chromosomes identical in number and structure to the original parent set collected together and ready to go into the two daughter cells.

Q (*a*) How many chromosomes will be together at each opposite pole above?
(*b*) How many different types of chromosomes will there be at each pole above?

A (*a*) 4 (*b*) 4

21 As the chromosomes are pulled towards the polar regions of the spindle by the centromere, they assume the typical U or V shapes of late anaphase.

Q Copy figure 120 from frame 20 but draw in the chromosomes as they would appear on approaching the poles.

A Your drawing should look like figure 121.

121 Late anaphase

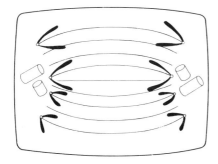

22 The final stage in mitosis is telophase, where the chromosomes reach the polar ends of the spindle and become densely packed. The nuclear envelopes form around them and nuclear division is complete.

Q (*a*) How many nuclei are present in the cell at the end of telophase?
(*b*) What follows telophase?

A (*a*) 2
(*b*) Cytokinesis, division of the cytoplasm.

23 *Summary frame*

Q Fill in the missing words below.

Mitosis consists of four phases: _____,
_____, _____ and _____. During prophase,

paired chromatids become attached to the _____ _____ at their centromeres and the _____ envelope breaks down. Metaphase follows, in which the chromatids assemble at the spindle _____ Then anaphase occurs, in which the centromere splits in two, and each of the pair of chromatids is drawn towards an opposite _____ by contraction of the spindle fibres. The final stage is called _____ in which the chromosomes reach the polar ends of the spindle and ____ envelopes are formed around them. It is important to remember that all of these stages are continuous and they are named and described separately only for convenience.

A Prophase, metaphase, anaphase, telophase, spindle fibres, nuclear, equator, pole, telophase, nuclear.

24 In both plant and animal cells, the division of the parent cell occurs across the equator region of the cell.

In plant cells, a new cell wall is laid down on the cell plate which is formed across the equator region of the spindle and then outwards to cut off the two daughter cells. In animal cells, the cell membrane cuts in across the equator region. Whilst this is happening, the spindle apparatus breaks down.

Q Which of the diagrams 122(*a*) and 122(*b*) represents cytokinesis in (*a*) animal, and (*b*) plant cells?

122 Cytokinesis

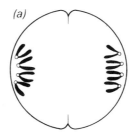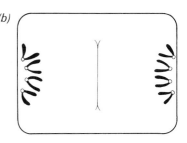

A 122(*a*) – animal cell, 122(*b*) – plant cell

8.5 Summary assignment 9

You may refer to any previous frames in completing this exercise.

123 Table for summary assignment 9

name	sketch	activity

Copy table 123 and then

1 List the names of the various stages of the mitotic cell cycle.

2 Describe the major activities of each stage.

3 Draw a sketch diagram to show the position of chromosomes, drawing nuclear division.

Show this work to your tutor.

Self test 11, page 87, covers sections 8.3 and 8.4 of this unit.

8.6 Multicellular organisms

You have seen that there is an upper limit to cell size, after which cells divide. If, instead of separating, these daughter cells remain together, a new level of organisation is reached.

With more than one cell present within the organism, each cell need no longer carry out all the life processes. Different cells may become specialised for different functions. Cells may specialise in feeding and pass food onto cells which specialise in support or defence or reproduction. Division of labour among cells makes an organism more efficient and increases the possiblity of its exploiting energy sources not available to simpler organisms.

However, specialisation usually means that there is loss of ability to perform some other function and reduces the chance of independent survival.

Although it seems possible that many types of cell would evolve, a microscopic examination of animal cells shows that they may be classified into about five main types. A similar situation exists among plants. (See figure 124.)

124 Plant and animal tissues

(a) Animal

	example
connective tissue	blood, bone, cartilage
epithelial tissue	outer layer of skin lining of gut and blood vessels
muscle tissue	voluntary, involuntary and heart muscle
nervous tissue	neurons, neuroglia
reproductive tissue	sperm, eggs

(b) Plant tissue

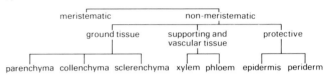

An association of cells of the same kind which work together to perform a common function is called a **tissue**. Organisation of cells into tissues is another structural advance because most functions of cells can be better performed by a group of cells of the same type acting together than by separate cells.

This stage in evolution can be demonstrated very well by a relatively simple animal, *Hydra*.

Practical I: Observing living *Hydra*

Materials

Hydra culture, cavity slide and cover-slips, microscope with × 4 and × 40 objectives and lamp, large aperture teat pipette, 5% solution of glycerine, methylene blue, *Daphnia* or brine shrimps (*Artemia*)

Procedure

(a) Place a living *Hydra* in a drop of water on a cavity slide and observe its movement under the × 4 objective. When left undisturbed, it expands so that its body and long crown of tentacles can be seen.

Disturb the water and watch the rapid shrinkage of both body and tentacles.

Record your observations by means of notes and labelled sketches.

(b) Lower a cover-slip onto the drop of water. Wait for the animal to extend and then examine the tentacles under high power.

Sketch what you can see. Do the tentacles appear warty? Each 'wart' is a tubercle containing a battery of nematocysts (stinging cells).

(c) The nematocysts are used for food capture. It is thought that the combined effect of chemical and contact stimuli is necessary to bring about the discharge of nematocysts. Remove the cover-slip. Add a few drops of 5% glycerine and some methylene blue and leave for a few minutes before replacing the cover-slip. The glycerine will provide chemical stimulation and the pressure exerted by the cover-slip the contact stimulation. The methylene blue should diffuse into the nematocysts so that they may be seen more clearly. Observe the tentacles under the HP objective and record your observations in notes and sketches.

(d) Does your *Hydra* have a bud? If so, make a sketch of what you can observe and annotate it.

(e) Collect a fresh *Hydra*. Allow it time to recover from handling and to expand its tentacles. See if you can observe its feeding or some of its reactions to food. Try adding a small crustacean, such as *Daphnia*, or a brine shrimp to the water. Again, record what you see. (*Hydra* may not respond to food under the conditions present on a slide.)

Show this work to your tutor.

The body wall of *Hydra* consists of an outer and inner layer of cells separated by a non-cellular, jelly-like layer called mesogloea. The cells of both layers have their bases drawn out into long, contractile muscle fibres which interlock with muscular fibres from other cells. **Ectoderm** fibres contract the animal lengthwise (shorten and thicken). **Endoderm fibres** run round the animal and lengthen and narrow the body when they contract. These two layers of cells are classed as tissues because there is a basic similarity in the shape of the cells and they have a common function. Apart from being considered as muscular tissue, the two layers of cells in *Hydra* can be thought of as epithelial tissue. An **epithelium** is a group of cells covering a free surface. The outer layer, or ectoderm may be thought of as a protective epithelium, while the inner layer, or endoderm, has similarities with a glandular epithelium. The cells of

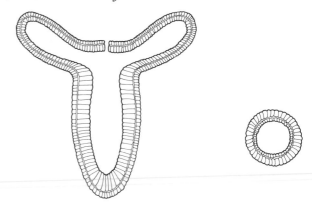

this layer are concerned chiefly with digestion. Some secrete enzymes which digest the prey to a thick suspension which is then engulfed by amoeboid cells which are also present.

The tissues of *Hydra* differ from the tissues of more complex animals because they perform more than one function. Also present in *Hydra* are interstitial cells which are unspecialised and retain the capacity to develop into other types as needed.

A network of nerve cells pass on stimuli received by sensory cells in both layers. Other cells are concerned with reproduction (ovary and testis).

8.7 Extension: The evolution of the earliest cells

Study the following paragraphs and diagrams from *The Evolution of the Earliest Cells* by J. William Schopf, Scientific American, September 1978.

Paragraphs 1, 2, 3 – p. 3
16, 17, 18, 19, 20, 21, 22 – pp. 5, 6, 7, diagram (p. 5)
48, 49 – p. 12, diagram (pp. 14, 15)
57, 58, 59, 60, 61, 62 – pp. 15, 16
71, 72, 73, 74 – p. 18, diagram (p. 17)

Answer the following questions.

1 How did genetic variation act as a 'mechanism of evolution'?

2 Which two important events are referred to as happening in the pre-Cambrian period?

3 Define the terms eukaryote and prokaryote. Give three differences and three similarities between eukaryotes and prokaryotes.

126 Diagram of *Hydra* showing cell types

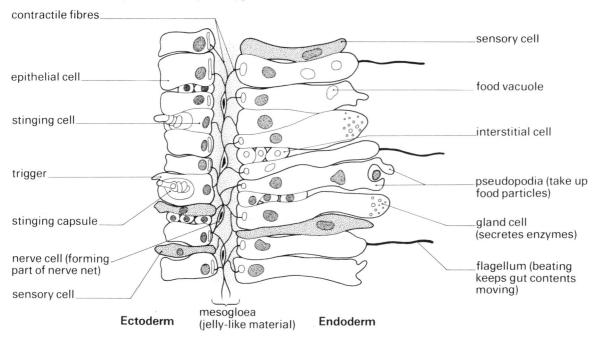

contractile fibres

epithelial cell

stinging cell

trigger

stinging capsule

nerve cell (forming
part of nerve net)

sensory cell

sensory cell

food vacuole

interstitial cell

pseudopodia (take up
food particles)

gland cell
(secretes enzymes)

flagellum (beating
keeps gut contents
moving)

Ectoderm   mesogloea
(jelly-like material)   **Endoderm**

4 Why does the author suspect that 'eukaryotic cells
have always been aerobic'.

5 Which developed first, eukaryotes or prokaryotes?
What evidence is there for your answer?

6 Explain the paradox of 'the anaerobic nature of
bacterial photosynthesis'.

7 When did anaerobic and aerobic prokaryotes arise?
What effects did aerobic prokaryotes have?

Show this work to your tutor.

Section 9 Self tests

Self test 1

1 Which one of the following sentences best describes the cell theory?
(a) The cells found in plants are very similar to those found in animals and this may indicate a common ancestor.
(b) The cells of unicellular organisms are different from those of multicellular organisms because they perform a whole range of activities and are not specialised.
(c) All animals and plants are built up from similar subunits which are called cells.
(d) All new individual organisms originate from the cells of parent individuals.

2 Which of the following organisms is not an exception to the cell theory?
(a) prokaryote (b) bacterium (c) blue-green alga
(d) *Amoeba*

3 Which of the following structures could an organism be without but still be described as conforming to the cell theory?
(a) cell wall (b) nucleus (c) cell membranes
(d) cytoplasm

4 Which of the following sentences best describes the difference between unicellular and multicellular organisms?
(a) A unicellular organism consists of one specialised cell whilst a multicellular organism has many specialised cells.
(b) A multicellular organism has more than one cell whilst a unicellular organism has no cell structure.
(c) A unicellular organism has one non-specialised cell whilst a multicellular organism has many specialised cells.
(d) A multicellular organism has many specialised cells whilst a unicellular organism has no cell structure.

Self test 2

1 Which of the following is the general formula for a carbohydrate?
(a) $(CH_2O)_n$ (b) $C_x(H_2O)_y$ (c) $C_xH_2O_y$
(d) $(C_6H_{12}O_6)_n$

2 Which of the molecules listed below could be involved in a glycosidic bond?
(a) amino acid (b) monosaccharide
(c) triglyceride (d) nucleic acid

3 Which of the following formulae represents a pentose monosaccharide?
(a) $C_6H_{12}O_6$ (b) $C_5H_{10}O_5$ (c) $C_4H_8O_4$ (d) $C_3H_6O_3$

4 Which monosaccharide is a triose monosaccharide?
(a) ribose (b) fructose (c) glucose (d) glyceraldehyde

5 How many carbon atoms are represented in the simplified structural formula of glucose shown in figure 127?

127 Simplified structural formula for glucose

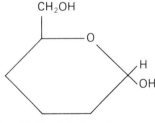

(a) 6 (b) 5 (c) 7 (d) 1

6 The structural formula for glucose (figure 127) represents α-glucose. In what way would β-glucose differ in its chemical composition from α-glucose?
(a) one less carbon atom
(b) two more hydrogen atoms
(c) one less oxygen atom
(d) no difference

7 The structural formula in figure 128 also represents a glucose. Which form is represented?

128 Structural formula for glucose

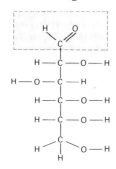

(a) ring form (b) furanose form (c) open chain form
(d) pyranose form

8 The shaded portion of the glucose structural
formula in figure 128 represents a particular chemical
group. What is this called?
(a) alpha (b) beta (c) aldehyde (d) keto

9 Most larger carbohydrates are based on the monosaccharides which are
(a) trioses. (b) hexoses. (c) pentoses. (d) sucroses.

10 Which of the following is a non-reducing
disaccharide?
(a) lactose (b) sucrose (c) maltose (d) glucose

11 Which formula below represents an amino acid?

$$(a) \quad \overset{\overset{R}{|}}{N}H-CH-COOH$$
$$(b) \quad \overset{\overset{R}{|}}{N}H_2-CH-COOH$$
$$(c) \quad \overset{\overset{R}{|}}{N}H_2-CH-COH$$
$$(d) \quad \overset{\overset{R}{|}}{N}H_3-CH-COOH$$

12 Which of the following amino acids has the
simplest R group?
(a) alanine   (b) glycine   (c) tyrosine   (d) valine

13 Which part of an amino acid is not involved in
peptide linkage?
(a) amino group (b) carboxyl group (c) R group
(d) all above are involved

14 Which of the following molecular weights is
unlikely to be representing a protein?
(a) 200 (b) 6000 (c) 70 000 (d) 473 000

15 In which type of protein would you expect the
polypeptide chains to be tightly folded?
(a) fibrous (b) globular (c) helical (d) colloidal

16 Which of the following levels of structure of a
protein corresponds to the sequence of amino acids in
a polypeptide chain?
(a) primary (b) secondary (c) tertiary (d) quarternary

17 The loss of a protein's characteristic properties
when subjected to extremes of pH or heat is referred
to as
(a) coagulation.   (b) denaturation.
(c) precipitation.   (d) deamination.

18 Which of the following types of linkage is least
likely to be involved in breakdown when the tertiary
structure of a protein is destroyed?
(a) hydrogen bond   (b) disulphide bridge
(c) peptide bond   (d) glycosidic bond

19 Which of the following lipids would be classified
as a simple lipid?
(a) waxes (b) phospholipid (c) glycolipid
(d) triglyceride

20 The main difference between a fat and an oil is
that
(a) at 20 °C fats are solid, oils are liquid.
(b) oils have no saturated bonds, fats do.
(c) at 80 °C fats are solid and oils are liquid.
(d) oils contain at least one phosphorus atom.

21 Simple lipids are made up from triglycerides
which consist of
(a) three fatty acids.
(b) one glycerol molecule and three fatty acids.
(c) three glycerol molecules and one fatty acid.
(d) three glycerol molecules.

22 A major difference between DNA and RNA is in
the type of
(a) peptide linkage.
(b) phosphoric acid.
(c) sugar.
(d) purine bases.

23 Which of the following is not a pyrimidine?
(a) thymine (b) cytosine (c) uracil (d) guanine

24 Which of the following statements about base specificity is true for DNA?
(*a*) Pyrimidines may bond with pyrimidines.
(*b*) Purines may bond with purines.
(*c*) Pyrimidines may bond with purines.
(*d*) All of the above are true for DNA.

Match the shapes **a, b, c, d** in figure 129 with

25 carbohydrate.

26 lipid.

27 protein.

28 nucleic acid.

129 Shapes of molecules

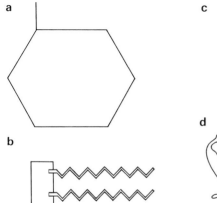

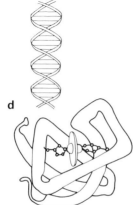

In which of the above would you expect to find

29 glycosidic bonds?

30 peptide linkages?

31 ester bonds?

32 pentose-phosphate linkages?

Match the following list of functions **33–40** with one only of
(*a*) carbohydrate, (*b*) lipid, (*c*) protein, (*d*) nucleic acid.

Functions

33 waterproofing

34 catalysis of biochemical reactions

35 hereditary material

36 oxygen transport

37 sweet taste

38 soluble in ether

39 fibrous

40 insoluble in water

Self test 3

Supply the missing words for the following passage:

Modern understanding of cell ultrastructure is based on studies with the **1** _____ microscope. This instrument has revealed much greater detail about structures barely visible using the light microscope and has led to the discovery of previously unknown structures such as **2** _____.

The cell nucleus with its densely staining region, the **3** _____, has been revealed to be contained by a **4** _____ plasma membrane with **5** _____ in it. These allow materials to pass between the cytoplasm and nucleoplasm. The cytoplasm is itself contained by a **6** _____ plasma membrane which acts as a barrier between the cell and its external environment. In some cells, this plasma membrane may be much folded to form **7** _____ which increase the surface area available for exchange of materials.

In plant cells, primary and secondary cellulose cell walls may be laid down on the cell membrane. These act as **8** _____ structures and, in some cases, the secondary wall, which is much thicker than the primary wall, may be impregnated with a waxy material to form an impermeable **9** _____.

Both animal and plant cells have fine strands of cytoplasm running between neighbouring cells. These are called **10** _____ in plant cells and **11** _____ in animal cells.

Contractile **12** _____ fibres, called microtubules, are found in cilia, flagella and centrioles. Cilia, which are found in large numbers on the outside of some types of cell, have a **13** _____ arrangement of microtubules as do **14** _____ which are much larger than cilia and normally occur in pairs or as a single organ of locomotion. Centrioles have a **15** _____ arrangement of microtubules and are associated with the formation of **16** _____ fibres during nuclear division. Centrioles are similar to the **17** _____ found at the base of cilia and flagella.

The cytoplasm of both plant and animals cells has a complex system of membranes called the endoplasmic reticulum running through it. Smooth and endoplasmic reticulum have **18** _____ cavities inside this membrane system whilst rough endoplasmic reticulum has **19** _____ cavities with ribosomes attached to the outer surface. The ribosomes are responsible for **20** _____ synthesis and those associated with rough endoplasmic reticulum are believed to manufacture secretory proteins which pass into the tubular cavity and then along these to the external environment. The **21** _____ _____ is a type of smooth endoplasmic reticulum which is associated with granule-containing vesicles. Smooth endoplasmic reticulum is believed to be involved in the manufacture of lipids and steroids. Chloroplasts and mitochondria are structures involved in **22** _____ metabolism. Chloroplasts are found in the green cells of plants and are **23** _____-shaped structures. They have a **24** _____ outer membrane enclosing a series of flattened membrane-like structures called **25** _____. These are arranged in stacks called **26** _____ which are embedded in the chloroplast stroma. Chloroplasts are responsible for photosynthesis. Mitochondria are spherical or rod-shaped structures responsible for **27** _____ which are found in both animal and plant cells. They have an outer single membrane enclosing an inner membrane which is folded into structures called **28** _____.
Finally, there are various types of vacuoles and vesicles in the cytoplasm of some cells. Pinocytic vesicles take in small particles or fluids into the cell whilst **29** _____ vesicles engulf larger particles. Lysosomes are vesicles which originate in the Golgi body and contain digestive **30** _____. **31** _____ vacuoles function as water pumps in certain animal cells controlling the discharge of excess water from the cell whilst mature plant cells have large **32** _____ vacuoles containing cell sap which play a major role in maintaining the shape and form of a plant cell.

Self test 4

1 Fill in the missing words below.

Energy is usually described as the capacity to do (*a*) _____ and is measured in (*b*) _____, represented by the symbol (*c*) _____. There are two main types of energy called (*d*) _____ and (*e*) _____. A boulder rolling down a hill represents (*f*) _____ energy, whilst a can of petrol represents (*g*) _____. The two main types of energy may occur in five different forms, chemical, mechanical, nuclear (*h*) _____ and (*i*) _____. A carbohydrate molecule represents a (*j*) _____ form of energy.

A petrol-driven car is an example of the conversion of (*k*) _____ into mechanical energy. When such conversions occur some energy is always converted into a useless form. This is in accordance with the (*l*) _____ law of thermodynamics. However, energy is never destroyed or lost in such conversions in accordance with the (*m*) _____ law of thermodynamics.

The energy which is available to do work in a chemical system is called the (*n*) _____ energy, represented by the symbol (*o*) _____. The amount of this energy in a system changes during chemical reactions involving the system. Such reactions are classified as (*p*) _____ if they result in a loss and (*q*) _____ if they result in a gain of such energy.

2 Figure 130 represents a chemical reaction with labels **A**, **B** and **C** relating to different quantities of energy.

130   Diagram for question 2

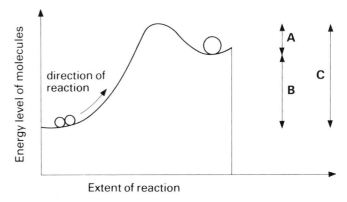

(*a*) Which quantity of energy is associated with (i) activation energy, (ii) energy barrier, (iii) ΔG?
(*b*) Which part of the following descriptions is more likely to apply to the above reaction?

(i) endergonic or exergonic
(ii) involving $-\Delta G$ or $+\Delta G$
(iii) reduction or oxidation
(iv) photosynthesis or respiration

3 Figure 131 represents a process of great importance in metabolism.
(*a*) Name the process.
(*b*) State the missing labels represented by **A** and **B**.

131   Diagram for question 3

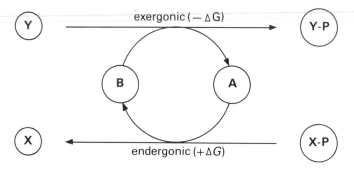

Self test 5

1 Indicate on the diagram of an amphipathic molecule (see figure 132)

132   Diagram for question 1

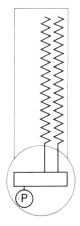

(*a*) the chemical name of the molecule represented.
(*b*) the chemical names of the different parts of the molecule.

(*c*) the hydrophilic and hydrophobic regions.
(*d*) How would such molecules behave in water?

2 Describe the appearance of the plasma membrane as seen by electron microscopy.

3 Give an explanation for the observation that fat solvents pass through the plasma membrane more rapidly than water solvents.

4 Give two reasons why the development of a membrane would be a major step in the evolution of the living cell.

5 What is the evidence that led to the proposal of a bilayer of lipid molecules in the plasma membrane?

6 Describe the structure of the plasma membrane according to the fluid mosaic model.

7 Describe two ways in which molecules can pass across a plasma membrane.

Self test 6

1 What is diffusion?

2 Name two factors which affect the rate of diffusion.

3 What is meant by a diffusion gradient?

4 Give an example of a biological diffusion gradient.

5 State two differences between active transport and diffusion.

Self test 7

1 Why is Visking tubing selected to act as a model to simulate cell membranes?

2 Explain osmosis in terms of diffusion.

3 Water passes into *Amoeba* constantly by osmosis, is collected in one place (contractile vacuole) and is expelled. What does this information tell us about the plasma membrane?

4 Many marine species of amoebae have no contractile vacuoles. How might this be related to the differing compositions of fresh water and sea water?

5 What is the name given to the membrane surrounding the vacuole of plant cells?

6 What will be the direction of water flow when a cell of solute potential of -300 kPa and pressure potential of 0 is immersed in a solution of solute potential of -100 kPa? Explain your answer.

7 Figure 133 represents the conditions present in two adjacent cells. In what direction would water flow between them? From **A** to **B** or from **B** to **A**? Explain your answer.

133 Diagram for question 7

A	B
$\psi_s = -500$ kPa	$\psi_s = -600$ kPa
$\psi_p = 300$ kPa	$\psi_p = 500$ kPa

8 Name the condition of a cell surrounded by pure water where the solute potential $= (100-x)$kPa and pressure potential $= x$ kPa (where x is a numerical value).

Self test 8

1 Define an activation threshold.

2 Explain why the activation energy of one molecule may be different from another.

3 What effect is an enzyme believed to have on energy barriers in reactions?

4 Sketch a graph which illustrates the different pathways available for a reaction which can be enzyme catalysed.

Self test 9

The series of graphs in figure 134 represent the general results from a series of investigations into the effect of varying conditions on enzyme activity.

Answer the following questions from these graphs.

1 (*a*) Describe the change in rate of enzyme reaction up to 58 °C.

134   Varying conditions and enzyme activity

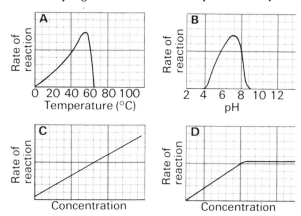

(*b*) What happens to the rate after 58 °C?
(*c*) Suggest an explanation for your observation in (*b*) above.
(*d*) Why is it incorrect to say that 58 °C is the optimum temperature for the enzyme in graph **A**?

2 In the varying pH investigation, a full range of pH's were tried.
(*a*) What is the effect of extremes of pH on enzyme reaction rates?
(*b*) What is the optimum pH for this enzyme?

3 (*a*) State what is being varied in concentration to produce (i) graph **C**, (ii) graph **D**.
(*b*) Describe generally the effect of increasing substrate concentration on the rate of enzyme reaction.
(*c*) What is the mathematical relationship between enzyme concentration and rate of reaction?

Self test 10

Enzymes are **1** _____ which act as very efficient biological **2** _____. This means that they become involved in biochemical reactions and **3** _____ the rate of such reactions without themselves being used up. They act by lowering the **4** _____ to a reaction thus lowering the **5** _____ energy needed by substrate molecules to react.

The conditions which prevail in a system affect the efficiency of enzymes. The rate of an enzyme-catalysed rection is **6** _____ proportional to the concentration of enzyme present and, at low substrate concentrations, the rate is directly proportional to **7** _____ concentrations. However, there is a limit to the rate at which a given concentration of enzyme can act and therefore at **8** _____ substrate concentrations the rate of an enzyme-catalysed reaction is constant. Usually enzymes exhibit catalytic activity only over a **9** _____ range of pH values. Within this range there will often be one particular pH value at which activity is greatest and this is known as the **10** _____ pH. The rate of reaction increases directly with temperature but only up to a **11** _____ temperature after which activity rapidly diminishes. The inactivation of enzymes by extremes of pH and temperature is called **12** _____ and is caused by the **13** _____ of the enzyme being irreversibly altered.

The shape of an enzyme is very important to its function. Substrate molecules fit into the **14** _____ of an enzyme like a lock fits with a **15** _____. Only certain molecules can fit into a particular active site and this accounts for the **16** _____ of enzymes – each one will only catalyse reactions involving one or a few chemically related substrates. Enzymes catalyse reactions in both directions and as they are always **17** _____ at the end of a reaction, they will continue doing so until their shape is changed and hence their activity lost.

Self test 11

1 Read through the following account of mitosis and then fill in the gaps with the most appropriate word or words to complete the account.

Mitosis is the division of a (*a*) _____ to give two (*b*) _____ of identical (*c*) _____ composition. During the first stage of this process, known as the (*d*) _____, the chromosomes shorten and (*e*) _____. They can also be seen to have separated lengthwise into (*f*) _____. The next stage of the process is marked by the membrane of the (*g*) _____ breaking down and the chromosomes moving towards the (*h*) _____ of the spindle. The chromosomes become attached to (*i*) _____ fibres. Meanwhile, the (*j*) _____ move apart initiating the drawing apart of the 'daughter' chromosomes towards the opposite

(*k*) _____ of the spindle. Each group of new chromosomes becomes part of a new nucleus and the chromosomes now become less easily (*l*) _____. In plant cells, a cell (*m*) _____ separates the two new cells, whilst in animal cells the (*n*) _____ cuts across between the nuclei.

2 Figure 135 represents a mitotic cell. Name the parts labelled **A, B, C** and **D**.

135 A mitotic cell

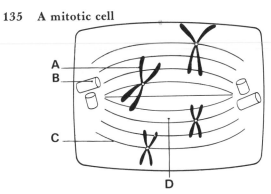

3 Draw a diagram of a cell showing four chromosomes at the metaphase stage of nuclear division. Label your diagram to show the equator and poles of the spindle apparatus.

4 The photomicrographs in figure 136 are of different stages of mitosis in onion cells. Indicate the name of each stage and place them in their correct sequence.

136 Photomicrographs of stages of mitosis in onion cells

Section 10 Answers to self tests

Self test 1

1 (*c*) **2** (*d*) **3** (*a*) **4** (*c*)

Self test 2

1 (*b*) **2** (*b*) **3** (*b*) **4** (*d*) **5** (*a*) **6** (*d*) **7** (*c*) **8** (*c*) **9** (*b*) **10** (*b*)
11 (*b*) **12** (*b*) **13** (*c*) **14** (*a*) **15** (*b*) **16** (*a*) **17** (*b*) **18** (*d*) **19** (*d*)
20 (*a*) **21** (*b*) **22** (*c*) **23** (*d*) **24** (*c*) **25** a **26** b **27** d **28** c **29** c
30 d **31** a **32** b **33** (*b*) **34** (*c*) **35** (*d*)

36 (*c*) **37** (*a*) **38** (*b*) **39** (*c*) **40** (*b*)

Self test 3

1 electron **2** ribosomes **3** nucleolus **4** double **5** pores
6 single **7** microvilli **8** supporting **9** cuticle
10 plasmodesmata **11** desmosomes **12** protein **13** 9 + 2
14 flagella **15** 9 × 3 **16** spindle **17** basal bodies
18 flattened **19** tubular **20** protein **21** Golgi body
22 carbohydrate **23** lens **24** double **25** lamellae
26 grana
27 respiration **28** cristae **29** phagocyte **30** enzymes
31 contractile **32** central

Self test 4

1 (*a*) work (*b*) joules (*c*) J (*d*)/(*e*) potential, kinetic
(*f*) kinetic (*g*) potential (*h*)/(*i*) radiant, electrical (*j*) chemical
(*k*) chemical (*l*) second (*m*) first (*n*) free (*o*) G (*p*) exergonic
(*q*) endergonic

2 (*a*) (i) C (ii) C (iii) B
(*b*) (i) endergonic (ii) $+\triangle G$ (iii) reduction (iv) photosynthesis

3 (*a*) energy coupling (*b*) (A) ATP (B) ADP

Self test 5

1 (*a*), (*b*) and (*c*) See figures 56 and 57, page 37.
(*d*) They would arrange themselves with their heads dissolved in the water and their tails sticking out of the
water.

2 Two dark lines separated by a lighter region.

3 The fat solvents can dissolve in the phospholipid and,
therefore, move through/between the molecules.

4 (*a*) It would allow a concentration of molecules which
would speed up metabolic reactions.
(*b*) It would prevent potentially harmful molecules entering
the cell.

5 The amount of lipid present in cell membranes was
sufficient to cater for double the known surface area of the
membranes.

6 A matrix of phospholipid molecules arranged in a
bilayer with globular protein molecules dissolved in the
matrix at irregular intervals.

7 By dissolving in and out of the phospholipid bilayer or
through the transmembrane channels of integrated
proteins.

Self test 6

1 Diffusion is the net movement of molecules from a
region of high concentration to a region of low concentration.

2 Temperature, concentration, size of molecule

3 The difference between the degree of concentration of a
substance in one area and the degree of concentration of
the substance in another area when it is possible for
diffusion to occur between the two areas.

4 (*a*) Oxygen in the lung and in the blood capillaries
surrounding the lung tissue.
(*b*) Soluble food in the small intestine and in the blood
capillaries surrounding it.

5 (*a*) Active transport requires energy input from the
biological system; diffusion is a passive physical process.
(*b*) Active transport may move substances from regions of
low concentration into regions of higher concentration;
diffusion is always from a region of high concentration to
a region of low concentration.

Self test 7

1 Visking tubing is a partially permeable membrane. The cell membrane is also partially permeable.

2 Osmosis is a special type of diffusion that occurs when two aqueous solutions of differing concentrations are separated by a partially permeable membrane. Larger solute molecules cannot pass through the membrane but the smaller water molecules diffuse from the region of their higher concentration (in the less concentrated solution) to the region of lower concentration of water molecules (more concentrated solution).

3 That (i) the plasma membrane acts as a partially permeable membrane, (ii) it can break and reform (to allow the rapid expulsion of water).

4 Sea water has a greater concentration of salts and may be equal in concentration to the cytoplasm of *Amoeba*, thus no osmosis may occur. Fresh water will always be very dilute, much more so than the cytoplasm of *Amoeba* and osmosis will be continuous.

5 Tonoplast.

6 Water will flow *into* the cell from the high water potential to the lower. (In this case, solute potential is identical to water potential as pressure potential is zero.)

7 From B to A.   Cell A $\psi = -500 + 300 = -200$
Cell B $\psi = -600 + 500 = -100$

8 Fully turgid

Self test 8

1 Activation energy is that amount of energy required by a molecule before it will undergo a reaction.

2 The activation energy of a molecule is the energy required to reach the activation energy threshold. As molecules of the same type have different energy levels, they will require different activation energies to reach the same threshold.

3 Enzymes are believed to lower energy barriers by opening a different pathway for the reaction.

4 Compare with figure 97.

Self test 9

1 (a) Rate of reaction is directly proportional to temperature.
(b) Rate decreases rapidly.
(c) The enzyme has been inactivated/denatured by the high temperature.
(d) Because it would not act at this rate for long due to denaturation and therefore the optimum must be at a lower rate for longer. It depends on the incubation time required.

2 (a) Complete inactivation of the enzymes causing zero rate of reaction.
(b) 7.2

3 (a) graph C – enzyme; graph D – substrate
(b) Reaction rate increases up to a maximum with increasing substrate concentration. After this point there is no further increase because enzyme molecules are all involved in catalytic activity at maximum rate.
(c) Directly proportional

Self test 10

1 proteins **2** catalysts **3** increase **4** energy barrier
5 activation **6** directly **7** substrate **8** excess **9** narrows
10 optimum **11** maximum **12** denaturation **13** shape
14 active site **15** key **16** specificity **17** regenerated

Self test 11

1 (a) nucleus (b) nuclei (c) nucleic acid (d) prophase
(e) thicken (f) chromatids (g) nucleus (h) equator
(i) spindle (j) centromere (k) poles (l) visible (m) plate
(n) membrane

2 A chromatid B centriole C spindle fibre D equator

3 See figure 137.

137   **Diagram for question 3**

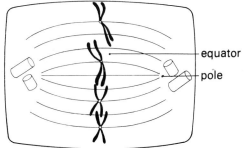

4 D early prophase C prophase A metaphase F early anaphase E anaphase B early telophase G interphase

Section 11 Answers to self-assessment questions

1 The three principles of cell theory are
(*a*) all living things are made up of cells;
(*b*) cells are capable of independent existence;
(*c*) cells can only arise from pre-existing cells.

2 A specialised cell is one which has developed a particular size, shape and chemistry suited to the specific function which it performs.

A multicellular organism is one which is composed of groups of specialised cells.

A unicellular organism consists of only one cell capable of carrying out all the necessary functions of life.

3 (*a*) Similarities – both plant and animal cells have a nucleus bounded by a nuclear membrane (with the exception of red blood cells), a cytoplasm containing cell organelles and a plasma membrane. Differences – plant cells have a cell wall and when mature they normally have a large central vacuole, whilst animal cells have no cell wall or central vacuole.
(*b*) A generalised cell is one which is constructed to represent the typical structure found in animal or plant cells.
(*c*) See figure 138.

138   A generalised animal cell

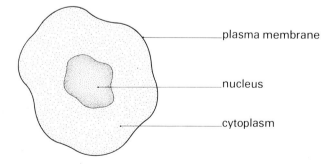

plasma membrane

nucleus

cytoplasm

4 (*a*) Bacteria (including blue-green bacteria) are exceptions to the cell theory because although they may be considered as living organisms they do not have a cellular structure. Both lack the membrane-enclosed nucleus which typifies cells.
(*b*) An *Amoeba* is typical of an animal cell in having a

plasma membrane, cytoplasm and membrane-enclosed nucleus. It therefore conforms with the cell theory.

5 A prokaryote example must be a bacterium whilst an eukaryote example could be any other organism.

6 (*a*) Activities observable in the film

(i) Movement
There are two aspects of movement: movement of the whole organism from place to place (locomotion) and movement within the organism. One or both aspects were displayed by all the organisms in the film. They were moving actively from place to place and, in addition, there was movement of the cytoplasm inside all the cells shown. This movement of cytoplasm within cells is called cyclosis.

(ii) Feeding (nutrition)
Feeding could be observed in *Amoeba* which engulfs food particles by flowing around them, and in *Paramecium*, which wafts food particles into its gullet using long, hair-like cilia. Feeding was not visible in *Euglena*.

(iii) Sensitivity
Living organisms are sensitive to changes in their environment. They respond to stimulation from outside. The feeding behaviour of *Amoeba* and *Paramecium* is one example of this, but other types of response were shown in the film loop. *Paramecium* was shown bumping into solid objects, backing away and moving off in another direction.

(iv) Reproduction
Reproduction was seen in *Amoeba* and *Paramecium*. *Amoeba* was shown reproducing asexually by division, while two *Paramecium* individuals were shown conjugating, a sexual form of reproduction.

(*b*) Activities not observable in the film

(i) Growth

(ii) Respiration
This is the process by which the energy contained in food is released for use by the cell. It takes place in all living organisms.

(iii) Excretion
Chemical reactions within cells (such as respiration)

produce chemical by-products which, if allowed to accumulate, would be toxic to the cell. The elimination of these materials from the organism is called excretion and it is characteristic of all living organisms.

7 (*a*) 1 mm = 1000 μm = 1 000 000 nm
(1 mm = 10^3 μm = 10^6 nm)
(*b*) A mitochondrion with a light microscope (longest dimension of 100 nm); a large molecule with an electron microscope (longest dimension of 1 nm).

8 (*a*) Wavelength is the distance between two successive peaks in a waveform.
(*b*) Resolving power is the minimum distance by which two points must be separated in order for them to be distinguishable.

9 (*a*) (i) A condenser focuses light onto a specimen.
(ii) An objective produces an image of the specimen.
(*b*) The use of an evacuated chamber means that living material cannot be viewed and also means that the non-living material to be viewed must be treated in various ways which could distort the structure of the specimen.

10 A nuclear envelope   E chloroplast
    B cell membrane   F nucleus
    C cell wall   G mitochondrion
    D vacuole

11 The central vacuole is missing in figure 14. This is because the electron micrograph is of a young plant cell and the central vacuole does not develop until the plant cell matures. A plant cell with a central vacuole will be seen later in the section.

12 (*a*) See figure 142.

(*b*) Plant cell has cell wall, chloroplasts but no Golgi body.
(*c*) The apparent size is 64 mm × 42 mm
The magnification is 3200

The true size is $\dfrac{64}{3200}$ mm × $\dfrac{42}{3200}$ mm

 = 20 μm × 13 μm

13 Yes. It is within the lower limit (0.1 μm) of the light microscope.

14 Chromatin fibres

15 The hereditary material consists of those molecules which are passed on from generation to generation and carry instructions for protein manufacture which will ensure the production of a new generation of like organisms.

16 Material for the making of new DNA molecules (nucleic acids) must pass into the nucleus and the ribosomes must pass out.

17 The nuclear envelope is a double membrane with pores. The cell membrane is single, without pores. However, they are functionally similar in acting as barriers.

18 The surface area available for absorption, secretion or excretion is much increased by folding leading to greater efficiency in these activites.

19 The secondary cell wall is thicker and more rigid than the primary cell wall and is laid down between the primary cell wall and cell membrane.

20 Apparent distance between cell membranes is about 16 mm. Magnification is × 3600.
Therefore real distance between cell membranes is

$$\frac{16}{3600} \times 10^6 \, \text{nm} \approx 4500 \, \text{nm}$$

21 (*a*) The outer ones only
(*b*) Nine pairs
(*c*) 18 – the central pair from the cilium or flagellum do not extend into the basal body.

22 20 (nine outer pairs and one central pair)

23 Basal bodies have nine pairs of microtubules whilst centrioles have nine groups of three microtubules. Basal bodies are involved in the production of cilia and flagella, whilst centrioles are involved in spindle production. Basal bodies are found close to the cell membrane surface, whilst centrioles are found in the cytoplasm often near the nucleus.

24 One difference between smooth and rough ER is the presence of ribosomes on rough ER and their absence on smooth. A similarity between smooth ER and the Golgi body is the flattened nature of the cavities.

25 Ribosomes originate from the nucleolus within the nucleus.

26 See figure 140.

27 (*a*) See figure 141.
(*b*) Mitochondria are involved in the formation of ATP molecules which act as sources of energy for certain reactions. The more active a cell is, the more energy its activities require, and the more mitochondria it needs to supply that energy in the form of ATP molecules.
(*c*) Chloroplasts and mitochondria are both organelles of cells, concerned with carbohydrate metabolism, have

139 Drawing of electron micrograph 15

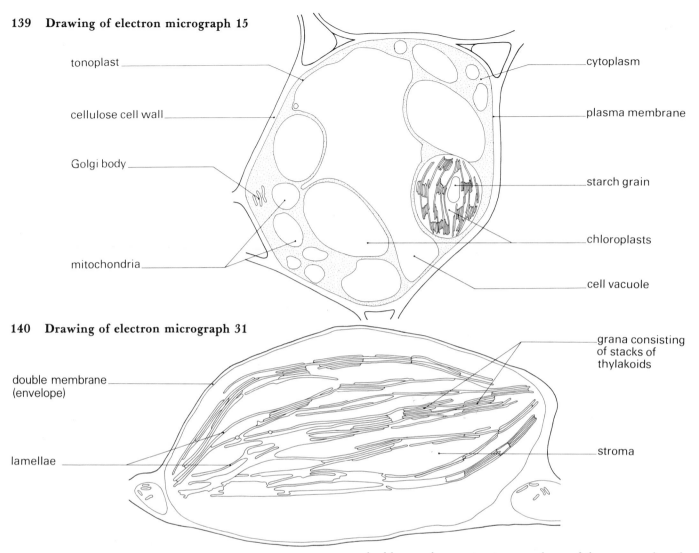

tonoplast

cellulose cell wall

Golgi body

mitochondria

cytoplasm

plasma membrane

starch grain

chloroplasts

cell vacuole

140 Drawing of electron micrograph 31

double membrane
(envelope)

lamellae

grana consisting
of stacks of
thylakoids

stroma

141 Drawing of electron micrograph 33

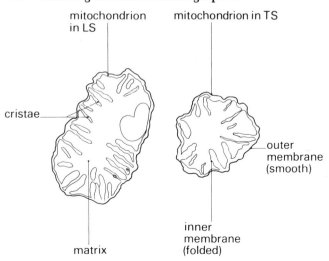

mitochondrion
in LS

mitochondrion in TS

cristae

outer
membrane
(smooth)

matrix

inner
membrane
(folded)

double membrane structures and are of the same order of magnitude. They differ in that chloroplasts are only found in plant cells, whilst mitochondria are found in all cells; chloroplasts are concerned with synthesis of carbohydrates and mitochondria with their breakdown. The inner membranes of chloroplasts are arranged in a much more complicated way than the finger- or shelf-like organisation in mitochondria and chloroplasts are generally lens-shaped whilst mitochondria are spherical or rod-shaped.

28 The vesicle membranes must be broken open in some way or the contents broken down or changed in structure so as to be able to diffuse across the membranes.

29 The lysosomes can be used in breaking down worn-out organelles and proteins, thus releasing raw materials from their structure for use elsewhere in the cell.

30 See figure 139

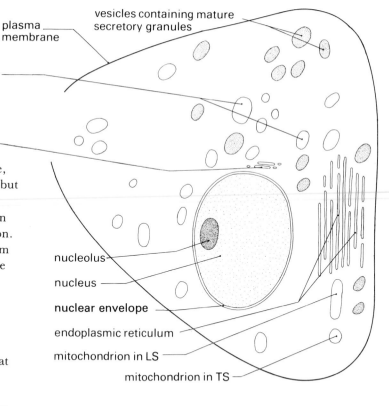

Labels on figure: plasma membrane; vesicles containing mature secretory granules; vesicles containing newly synthesised granules; Golgi body; nucleolus; nucleus; **nuclear envelope**; endoplasmic reticulum; mitochondrion in LS; mitochondrion in TS

31 (*a*) An atmosphere containing such gases as methane, ammonia, cyanogen, carbon dioxide and water vapour but no gaseous oxygen.
(*b*) Large areas covered by warm, mineral-rich oceans in which the atmospheric gases would be present in solution.
(*c*) A variety of energy sources: ultraviolet radiation from the sun, heat from volcanic activity and electricity in the form of lightning.

32 Gaseous oxygen could reduce these large molecules back to their simple constituents.

33 (*a*) To remove the air so that the correct balance of gases could be achieved and, in particular, to ensure that no gaseous oxygen was present.
(*b*) The boiling water provides water vapour and also encourages circulation of the gases in the apparatus. The cooling jacket condenses the water vapour allowing any products formed in the reaction chamber to be collected in solution.
(*c*) Electrical
(*d*) Similar

34 (*a*) Amino acids, fatty acids, sugars and nucleic acids.
(*b*) These laboratory syntheses show that reactions take place in simulated 'primitive atmospheres' which produce the basic chemicals of life. They do not prove that similar events have ever taken place in nature but do support the hypothesis.

35 Proteins from amino acids, fats from fatty acids, carbohydrates from sugars and nucleic acids from nucleotides.

36 Coacervates help to bring together different molecules and keep them isolated to some extent from the external environment. Their molecules are therefore more likely to combine to form larger molecules or complexes and to this extent the coacervate is a simple form of pre-cell.

37 Your answers should be along the same lines as these.

(*a*) For two main reasons. Each new advance in the theory was preceded by a development in technology. The theory was therefore held back by, and was dependent upon, technology which took many years to develop.

Secondly, the theory was limited by contemporary ideas about the origin of life and living things. For example, when the theories of spontaneous generation and pre-existence were fashionable, scientists had little intellectual incentive to expand their observations about cells into a theory that accounted for the existence of these cells.

(*b*) They believed that new cells arose from living material just as crystals arise from a concentrated solution.

(*c*) The electron microscope

38 Your answers should be on the following lines.

(*a*) Pre-cells required energy for the following:
(i) for the synthesis of complex molecules (e.g. proteins from amino acids), (ii) for growth, (iii) for replacement of worn-out parts and (iv) for reproduction.

(*b*) Heat, lightning, ultraviolet light, and from chemical reactions.

(*c*) From chemical reactions, because it was in continual supply and also it would not destroy pre-cells.

(*d*) (i) A heterotroph is an organism that takes in organic molecules which are used as food. Animals are examples of heterotrophs.
(ii) An autotroph manufactures its own food from simple inorganic sources. Green plants are examples of autotrophs.

(e) They obtain energy from certain chemical reactions in the cell, notably those involving glucose.

39 If a molecule is soluble in the material of the membrane, it might be expected to pass through it more rapidly than if it was insoluble. This suggests that lipids are present in the cell membrane.

40 The phospholipid has only two fatty acid chains rather than the three found in a triglyceride. The site at which the third group is attached in a triglyceride is occupied by a phosphate group in the phospholipid.

41 The soluble heads would dissolve in the water and the tails would stick out from the surface because they are insoluble (see figure 58).

42 (a) (i) Red blood cells can easily be obtained in large quantities.
(ii) Red blood cells can be easily counted.
(iii) Red blood cells have a regular structure, therefore it is easy to measure their surface area.
(iv) Red blood cells are very simple in structure and all the lipid is in the cell membrane.
(b) You would expect to find sufficient lipids to form the total surface area of the red blood cells.

43 (a) The surface area of lipid molecules is twice that of the cell surface area.

Surface area of cells in 1 cm^3 of blood is

$$4.74 \times 10^9 \times 99.4 \ \mu m^2$$

$$= 471 \times 10^9 \ \mu m^2$$

$$= 0.471 \ m^2$$

Therefore the ratio of lipid to cell surface area

$$= \frac{0.92}{0.47} \approx 2:1$$

(b) A double layer of lipid molecules forms the cell membrane.

44 Cell membranes would have to be isolated and then chemically analysed to determine the types and quantities of substances present. Testing the arrangement of these molecules within the membrane is more difficult. One technique could be to label the lipids and proteins in the membrane. By suitable photographic techniques, the distribution of these molecules in the membrane could be seen under the electron microscope.

45 (a) The structure appears as two dark lines separated by a lighter region.

(b) The dark lines measure approximately 0.5 mm and the lighter region 1 mm. Therefore, at 200 000 times magnification

$$\text{dark line} \approx \frac{0.5}{200\ 000} \ nm = \frac{0.5 \times 10^6}{200\ 000} \ nm = 2.5 \ nm$$

light line ≈ 5 nm

therefore total width ≈ 10 nm

(c) They are of roughly the right order of size and proportion. More accurate measurements are possible, of course, and these did support Danielli and Davson's prediction and, therefore, their original hypothesis.

46 The phospholipids were completely isolated from water by the protein layer but ideally the hydrophilic parts should be in contact.

47 (a) The fluid mosaic model has its protein component embedded in the phospholipid bilayer at intervals and not completely covering the bilayer as in the Danielli–Davson model.
(b) The hydrophilic parts of the phospholipids are in contact with water molecules rather than cut off by a protein covering.

48 They called it fluid because it appears to have the properties of a fluid rather than a solid structure; parts of it move around, such as the protein component which can move through the phospholipid component. It is called a mosaic model because it is a pattern formed by different pieces, the phospholipids and proteins.

49 (a) Diffusion will stop when there is no longer any difference in concentration between the different areas of the container.
(b) Molecules never stop moving. When diffusion has stopped only net movement has stopped. That means that there are no more molecules moving in one direction than any other.

50 All of these factors affect the rate of diffusion.
(a) The bigger the size, the slower the rate due to friction between molecules.
(b) The higher the temperature, the faster the rate due to increased kinetic energy.
(c) The higher the concentration difference, the faster the rate due to more molecules being available to move in one direction rather than the other.
(d) Diffusion is very much faster in a gas than in a liquid. This is due to a number of factors. One of the most important is the distance between the molecules of the medium. Molecules of a gas are further apart than those in a liquid. Various forces of attraction, such as the

143 Time taken by different concentrations of ammonia molecules to diffuse along a tube

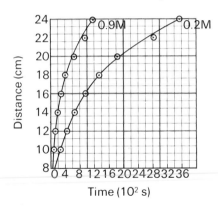

polarity of water molecules, may hold groups of water molecules together. It is estimated that molecules may diffuse through air about 10 000 times more rapidly than through water.

51 (a) The factor under investigation is the difference in concentration between two regions. Note that it is not the concentration of molecules in one region alone although this investigation was set up for convenience using only different concentrations of ammonia at one end of the tube.
(b) See figure 143.
(c) The molecules move due to their inherent kinetic energy. Because there are more molecules in highly concentrated regions than relatively lowly concentrated ones, there will be a net movement of molecules, purely by chance, from high to low concentrations. Air currents and convection currents are ruled out because the apparatus is sealed from these.
(d) The higher the concentration the more molecules will be moving away, diffusing from that region. Therefore, the net movement of molecules occurs more rapidly from higher concentrations than lower ones.
(e) 8–10 cm takes 28 s, 18–20 cm takes 235 s.
As the molecules diffuse away from the cotton wool their concentration gets less and less, and therefore the time taken for sufficient molecules to travel each 2 cm and change the litmus paper gets longer and longer.
(f) (i) The size of molecules – compare rates for two different substances of different molecular size both of which affect litmus paper.
(ii) The temperature – run investigation using solutions of same concentration at different temperatures.
(iii) Medium for diffusion – run the investigation filling the tube with different media, for instance gelatine.

52 Fastest in graph 3, slowest in graph 2.

53 The internal kinetic energy of the molecules. Remember that this movement is described as passive not because energy is not involved but because external energy is not involved.

54 (a) Transport by diffusion across cell membranes occurs when substances dissolve in and out of the lipid component of the membrane or when they pass through channels in the protein component.
(b) Some substances may also pass through the membrane without energy expenditure when they react with proteins in the membrane which transport them with the concentration gradient.

55 Active transport

56 (a) Molarity of sucrose bringing about no change in weight = 0.29–0.30 mol dm^{-3}

(b) Water potential of tissue is -810 kPa

57 (a) See graph 144.

144 Percentage of plasmolysed cells in different concentrations of sucrose solution

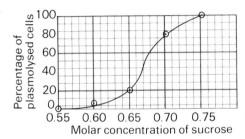

(b) 0.67 mol dm^{-3} (approximately)
(c) At point of incipient plasmolysis (i.e. 50% plasmolysis).

58 (a) The control set-up would be one in which normal blood cells were observed, that is in a solution of the same concentration as blood plasma.
(b) Hypertonic solution – net movement of water molecules out of the cell causing shrinking of the cells. Isotonic – no change in cell size, this indicates a balanced movement of water molecules.
Hypotonic – net movement of water molecules into the cells causing disruption of them as they swell. Only cell fragments are visible therefore.

59 This mechanism reduces the range of habitat suitable for a cell because its cytoplasm cannot be diluted beyond a certain limit without becoming inefficient.

60 (a) Having an impermeable layer resisting osmosis.
(b) Coping with the problem by some active compensating mechanism.

61 Organisms with impermeable outer layer must find

Some method of exchanging materials with the environment.

62 It would not in freshwater because the water potential of the water would always be higher than that of the animal cell. The cell would eventually burst.

63 See figure 145.

145 The boulder analogy

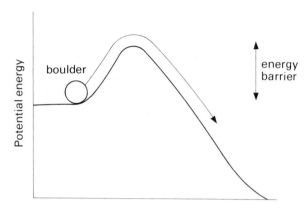

64 Activation energy

65 Only the molecule with an energy level of 8 in figure 96.

66 Because of the damage done to organic molecules by high temperatures.

67 (a) One unit
(b) The molecules with an energy level of 7 would have broken down without collision.

68 Because otherwise the rate of reaction would eventually be limited by the low amount of substrate present. Ultimately, with little substrate left, it would approach zero.

69 They should be as short as possible so as to allow measurement of the initial rate and avoid any tailing-off effect. If this is not possible, the investigation time must be mentioned in any statement of rate.

70 Because of the 'tailing-off' effect due to incubation time.

71 (a) A 2.9, B 8.8
(b) No. They have very different optimum pH values and would therefore be associated with different parts of the gut where such pH values were found. Enzyme A is found in the acidic stomach and enzyme B in the alkaline small intestine.

72 45 °C

73 If an enzyme was required to act for only a short time at a high rate, its optimum temperature might be higher than if it was required for a longer time at a lower rate.

74 (a) Keys are good at opening locks quickly. Alternative methods (gelignite) require extremes of physical conditions (explosions) or a lot longer time (lock-picking).
(b) Keys will only open one type of lock or a group of similar types.
(c) If a key's shape is changed, it will not open the lock.
(d) Keys can lock and unlock.
(e) Keys do not wear out.

75 (a) Ensure that the molecules are at the correct angle for reaction.
(b) Provide an alternative reaction pathway having a lower activation energy threshold.

76 In the lock-key model, the substrate molecules must make contact in a very precise manner to 'fit' the active site but with the induced-fit model, as long as they make contact with the active site of the enzyme, it will change shape to accommodate the substrate.

77 See table 146

146 Table for SAQ 77

Length of side of cell (units)	Surface area	Volume	Ratio surface area:volume
1	6	1	6:1
2	24	8	3:1
3	54	27	2:1

78 Greater

79 The same type of limitation on nuclear size would apply because the nucleus carries out all its exchanges with the cytoplasm across the nuclear envelope. Therefore, there is a limit to the size of the nucleus which its nuclear envelope can deal with efficiently. This limitation would also limit cell size because if a cell grew larger whilst the nucleus stayed the same size, there would be problems of control as the outer regions of the cell became distant from the nucleus.

Index